The Danube

The Danube
2,000 Years of History, Myth, and Legend

by Joseph Wechsberg

and the Editors of Newsweek Books

with photographs by Marvin E. Newman

Newsweek Books, New York

TITLE PAGE: *The picturesque city of Passau, last settlement on the German Danube, sits astride the confluence of two of the river's tributaries—the tiny Ilz, which arcs off to the far right, and the broad but shallow Inn, visible on the far left.*

Printed in the United States of America
First Edition 1979

Library of Congress Cataloging in Publication Data

Wechsberg, Joseph, 1907-

    The Danube: 2,000 Years of History, Myth and Legend

    Bibliography: p.
    Includes index.

    1. Danube Valley—History.
    2. Danube River—Description and travel—Views.
    I. Newsweek, Inc. Book Division.
    II. Title.

DB446.W37   943'.48   79-4720
ISBN 0-88225-273-9

Contents

SILESIA

POLAND

Breslau
Czestochowa
Dresden
Karl-Marx Stadt
Katowice
Ostrava

GERMAN
DEMOCRATIC REPUBLIC

Vltava

Cologne
Bonn

HESSE

Prague

CZECHOSLOVAKIA

Frankfurt

BOHEMIA
MORAVIA
Brno

Rhine

THE
PALATINATE

FRANCONIA

FEDERAL REPUBLIC

OF GERMANY

Nürnberg

Naab
Regen
BOHEMIAN FOREST

Pilsen

Regensburg
Straubing
Deggendorf
Ilz
Danube
March

Vah

Hron

Stuttgart

Altmühl

Donauwörth
Ingolstadt
Passau
Engelhartszell
Dürnstein
WACHAU VALLEY
Vienna

GALICIA
Strasbourg

BLACK FOREST

SWABIA

BAVARIA

Inn

Linz
Grein
Melk
Ybbs
Bratislava

FRANCE

Brigach
Brege

Sigmaringen

Blindheim
Augsburg
LECHFELD
Munich
BAVARIAN PLATEAU

Baden
Wiener Neustadt

Esztergom
Vác
Viségrad

Donaueschingen

Ulm

Iller

Traun

Nitra

Basel

Lake
Constance

Constance
Zürich

JURA MTS.

Lech
Isar

Innsbruck
TYROL

AUSTRIA

Salzburg

Enns

STYRIA

Graz

BURGENLAND

Leitha
Győr

Lake Neusiedler
Rába

BAKONY FOREST

Budapest

Danube

Bern

SWITZERLAND

Lucerne

LICHTENSTEIN

ALPS

CARINTHIA

Mur

SLOVENIA

Dunaujváros

Sió

Lake
Balaton

Kalosca

Milan

Lago di Garda

Zagreb

CROATIA

Drava

Baja
Pécs
Mohács

Turin

ITALY

Venice

Trieste

Rijeka

Sava

BOSNIA

Osijek
Vukova

Po

APENNINES

Bologna

ADRIATIC

DINARIC ALPS

YUGO

Genoa

Nice

Florence

LIGURIAN

SEA

SEA

Split

Sarajevo

HERZEGOVINA
ALPS
MON

Corsica

Dubrovnik

The Danube River

★ *Sources of the Danube*

0   50   100   150 Miles

1
Europe's River of Destiny

*T*he Danube has always meant many things to many men, its faces as varied as those of the peoples who have settled its banks, plied its waters, and sought to harness its power. To poets, the river has been an enduring source of inspiration, one steeped in myth and legend. To warriors, it was a highway to conquest for more than two thousand years. To merchants, it remains the Continent's major east-west waterway for the exchange of goods. Historians recognize the Danube Basin as one of the oldest, most fascinating civilized regions on earth, and statesmen acknowledge it as both the breeding ground of promise and the burial ground of failure. Owing to the genius of Johann Strauss, who used the sentimental lyrics of a forgotten Austro-Hungarian poet to write the river's theme song, it will always be known as "The Blue Danube." In truth, the Danube reflects many colors, politically as well as visually, but it is almost never blue.

The banks of the Danube, inhabited since the dawn of history, have witnessed millennia of immigration, occupation, and emigration. Some groups —the Huns, Goths, Avars, Slavs, Turks—moved westward; others—the Romans, Franks, Bavarians—moved eastward. The Romans called the river Danubius, a masculine name, but their successors, almost without exception, have thought of the river as feminine: in the German language she is the Donau; in Czech and Slovak, the Dunaj; in Hungarian, Duna; in Yugoslav and Bulgarian, Dunav; in Romanian, Dunarea; and in Russian, Dunay.

Statistics, no matter how impressive, rarely tell the full story. The Danube is 1,776 miles long—in Europe, only the Volga surpasses it in length and drainage area—but this hardly compares with the Nile's 4,132 miles or the Amazon's 4,000. The Danube can claim neither the deepest gorge nor the highest waterfall, yet more than any other river in Europe it is the reflection and escort of the Continent's fate. German romanticists call the Rhine their country's *Schicksalsfluss,* "river of destiny," but no European river has seen more victories and defeats, more violence and disaster, more shame and glory than the Danube. Trajan or Marcus Aurelius, Attila the Hun or Suleiman the Magnificent, Prince Eugene of Savoy or the first duke of Marlborough—the mighty river never belonged to one ruler; it was always a barrier to be conquered or a boundary to be defended.

Geographically, the Danube, with its more than three hundred tributaries, is divided into three sections. The upper river, which begins in West Germany's Black Forest, ends at Bratislava on the border of present-day Austria and Czechoslovakia. The middle section runs through Hungary and Yugoslavia to the Iron Gate, a point near the Bulgarian border where the river suddenly narrows from more than a mile to a mere two hundred yards, escaping the embrace of the Carpathian Mountains in a welter of dangerous currents and roiling water. The lower section of the Danube—for 300 of its 450 miles the border between Bulgaria and Romania—is slow and serene, meandering through vast, reed-choked marshes as it makes its languorous way to the Black Sea.

More meaningful is the tripartite manner in which historians divide the river. They speak of the German Danube, youthful and often picturesque, that ends at Passau; the Habsburg Danube, which takes its name from an empire that endured for almost eight hundred years and at one time stretched from the border of czarist Russia to the Adriatic Sea; and, finally, the Red Danube, which has existed only since 1945, when the Soviet Union, which actually controls only the last three miles of the waterway, became master of the river's destiny.

Long a spectator to history, the Danube itself has been thoroughly explored. Almost everything is known about the river except its exact source. Two brooks, the Brege and the Brigach, tumbling down the southern slopes of the Black Forest, join at the village of Donaueschingen. Only at the confluence, thirty miles below the tiny source of the Brege, are the waters officially called the Danube, although at that point their long journey is well underway. The Brege arises some 2,250 feet above sea level on the edge of a dense pine forest near the cuckoo-clock-making town of Furtwangen. The owner of the source itself, a physician from Würzburg, has erected a stone tablet bearing an official, framed announcement that this is the source "farthest away from the mouth of the Danube." So phrased, his assertion is indisputable, but the princes of Fürstenberg, who own nearly everything in Donaueschingen, also claim to own the great river's true source, which they say is located in the park attached to their castle. Tourists visiting the castle have themselves photographed near a tiny pool, surrounded by a fake baroque stone railing, called Donauquelle, Danube spring. Many pause to throw a good-luck coin into the pool before buying postcards and souvenirs of this more aristocratic source.

The infant Danube, freshly baptized at Donaueschingen, is a precocious child. Near Immendingen, a mere fifteen miles away, it suddenly disappears into the ground, percolates through the earth, and reappears several miles farther down. Below Fridengen, however, the river at last finds its identity and cuts a deep gorge through the rocks of the Swabian Jura. And below the Benedictine monastery of Beuron the Danube enjoys its first moment of grandeur as it passes beneath perpendicular cliffs crowned by medieval castles. At Sigmaringen, the finest of the upper Danube castles, that of the Hohenzollerns, rises almost magically from the water. The Prus-

The headwaters of the Brege (above), a tiny Alpine freshet that feeds into the Danube at Donaueschingen, Germany, are often said to mark the true source of the great river. But it is only at Donaueschingen that the waters of the Brege—commingled with those of the Brigach and fortified by a natural spring (top) located in the park of a princely palace—take the name Danube.

The mighty Danube, Europe's second longest river, begins its 1,776-mile journey to the Black Sea in the fastnesses of the Black Forest. There, on the deeply wooded flanks of the Bavarian Alps, the crystalline streams that form the infant Danube cascade down rocky escarpments and spill out across sunlit upland leas. These are the first of some three hundred tributaries that ultimately join the Danube—and they are unquestionably the most important. Without them the newborn river, weakened by mysterious seepages that siphon away its waters and sap its strength, might disappear altogether.

11

sian Hohenzollerns, whom we associate with Frederick the Great and the Kaiser, were Protestants; their cousins in Sigmaringen remained Catholics. In 1866 a member of the family, Carol I, was elected prince of Romania. Initially Germany's Iron Chancellor, Otto von Bismarck, was delighted to have "his man in Bucharest," someone who could be expected to promote Germany's interests in the Balkans. Later he was dismayed when Romania sided against Austria-Hungary and Germany in World War I. And still later, on a summer day in 1944, the Hohenzollern-Sigmaringen were ordered out of their castle by the Nazis, who wished to make room there for the leaders of Vichy France. Elderly residents of the village still remember Marshal Pétain, who refused to walk in the castle park because he considered himself a prisoner.

Farther downstream, at Ulm, the Danube becomes a respectable river. Here it is met by its first major tributary, the Iller, and here too it becomes navigable to hundred-ton craft. Ulmers are particularly proud of their beautiful Gothic cathedral, which was built over a period of a hundred years by the burghers of the town with no financial help from emperors, kings, or bishops. Ulm Cathedral has the world's highest church tower, which is, at 528 feet, thirteen feet higher than the spires of Cologne's Dom. A sign near the bank of the Danube says: "From Ulm, German settlers sailed on the Danube in the eighteenth century to southeastern Europe. Their descendants, expelled from their homes, returned after World War II to the land of their forefathers." This plaque records the fact that after Prince Eugene of Savoy defeated the Turks in 1717 and gained for the Habsburgs the lands known today as Hungary, Yugoslavia, and Romania, the Danube Swabians—including people from Swabia, the Palatinate, and Alsace—boarded ships in Ulm and went downstream to an uncertain future. They worked hard, became prosperous, and founded villages and towns in the Balkans. Some returned after World War I, however, and many more did so during the chaos following the collapse of the Nazi regime.

The Ulmers learned how to build ships from the Viennese. Later they reciprocated by helping defend Vienna against the Turks—both in 1529, during the first siege, and again in 1683, when many joined the allied forces of Duke Charles of Lorraine and the Polish king, John III Sobieski, that broke the second siege. Still later "Danube boatmen" from Ulm traveled all the way down to Belgrade. On October 18, 1745, Empress Maria Theresa and her husband Francis I, who had just been crowned Holy Roman emperor in Frankfurt, boarded a ship in Ulm and sailed triumphantly downstream to Vienna, their glittering capital.

The city made history again in 1805 when Napoleon, also a newly crowned emperor, brought his armies there to fight the Austrians. The Austrian commander, Baron Karl Mack von Leiberich of Bavaria, had been

Sigmaringen Castle, ancient seat of the Hohenzollerns and one-time residence of Marshal Pétain, casts its long shadow across a tranquil, weed-choked stretch of the upper Danube.

13

described by Archduke Charles, brother of Emperor Francis II, as a man whose "imbecility and conceit prevent him from even seeing difficulties." Napoleon, to whom Mack surrendered an army of 20,000 men, simply called him a charlatan.

After his victory at Ulm, Napoleon occupied Vienna, defeated the Austrians and their Russian allies at Austerlitz in December, 1805, and then dictated the peace treaty of Pressburg (now Bratislava in Czechoslovakia), a complex document that, among other things, gave him Venetia, Bavaria, and the Tyrol. The next year the Holy Roman Empire ceased to exist and Emperor Francis II became, more modestly, Francis I, hereditary emperor of the sprawling Austrian empire.

A few miles below Ulm is Blindheim (known as Blenheim in the English-speaking world), where the duke of Marlborough defeated the numerically stronger forces of Louis XIV and his Bavarian allies in August, 1704. Justly called one of the most decisive battles in history, Blenheim halted the march of Louis XIV and the expansion of autocracy. Marlborough's right-flank commander was Prince Eugene of Savoy, who had earlier offered his service to the Sun King. He was turned down, according to Duchess Liselotte von der Pfalz, because Louis XIV loved elegance and beauty and Prince Eugene was "small and ugly." Marlborough's forces

The world's tallest church steeple commands the skyline of Ulm (far left), a seemingly ageless medieval town that overlooks the confluence of the Danube and its first major tributary, the Iller. A second, much smaller river, the Blue, also enters the Danube at Ulm—but only after wending its way through the city's most picturesque section, the Fishermen's Quarter, which is visible at near left through the tracery of the cathedral's spire. In Ulm's open-air market, as old as the city itself, an elderly woman (below) sells cut flowers.

The first duke of Marlborough's stunning victory at Blenheim is celebrated in this enormous tapestry commemorating his triumph over the French on the banks of the Danube.

killed 12,000 French and captured 14,000 while suffering only 5,000 casualties. Thousands of French were said to have drowned in the Danube, which is difficult to reconcile with the fact that near Blenheim the river is peaceful and has no dangerous whirlpools.

The idyllic countryside of the upper Danube is deceiving; this fairy-tale land of castles and abbeys was a key battlefield during the Thirty Years' War, from 1618 to 1648. Donauwörth was besieged in 1632 by King Gustavus Adolphus of Sweden, and the same year Ingolstadt witnessed the death of the Catholic League's military commander, Johan von Tilly. The mystical power of the Counter-Reformation is beautifully expressed in Ingolstadt's Church of Maria de Victoria, the masterpiece of architect and painter Cosmas Damian Asam and his sculptor-brother Egid Quirin Asam, two great baroque and rococo artists. Saint Peter Canisius made the city's Jesuit university a citadel of the Counter-Reformation, and according to local legend Doctor Faust studied the "magical arts" in Ingolstadt.

After Ingolstadt, the Danube, already swollen by the Lech, flows into a dramatic gorge that cuts through four-hundred-foot cliffs surmounted by dark woods. At Kelheim, thirty miles below Ingolstadt, the Danube is joined by another major tributary, the Altmühl, the southern terminus of the Rhine-Main Canal. Low-draught tugs and barges, loaded in the Netherlands, reach Kelheim by way of the Rhine—and from there they can follow the Danube all the way to the Black Sea, traversing all of Central Europe by water. Louis I, the king of Bavaria whose affair with the notorious dancer and courtesan Lola Montez scandalized mid-nineteenth-century

By 1600, the Jesuit university at Ingolstadt (far left) had become a gathering place for the greatest thinkers of the Counter-Reformation. The city, which lies at the geographical heart of Bavaria, had also become a haven for talented and dedicated artists, one of whom spent thirty years commemorating the battle of Lepanto in the yard-high monstrance at near left. A supreme example of Bavarian baroque, the Church of Maria de Victoria (right) is Ingolstadt's architectural capstone. Its vast, perfectly flat ceiling—painted in a scant six weeks—is an unparalleled achievement in optical illusion.

OVERLEAF: Below Ingolstadt, the Danube cuts deep through the green Franconian Jura, exposing the chalk-white rock beneath, sometimes to a depth of more than four hundred feet.

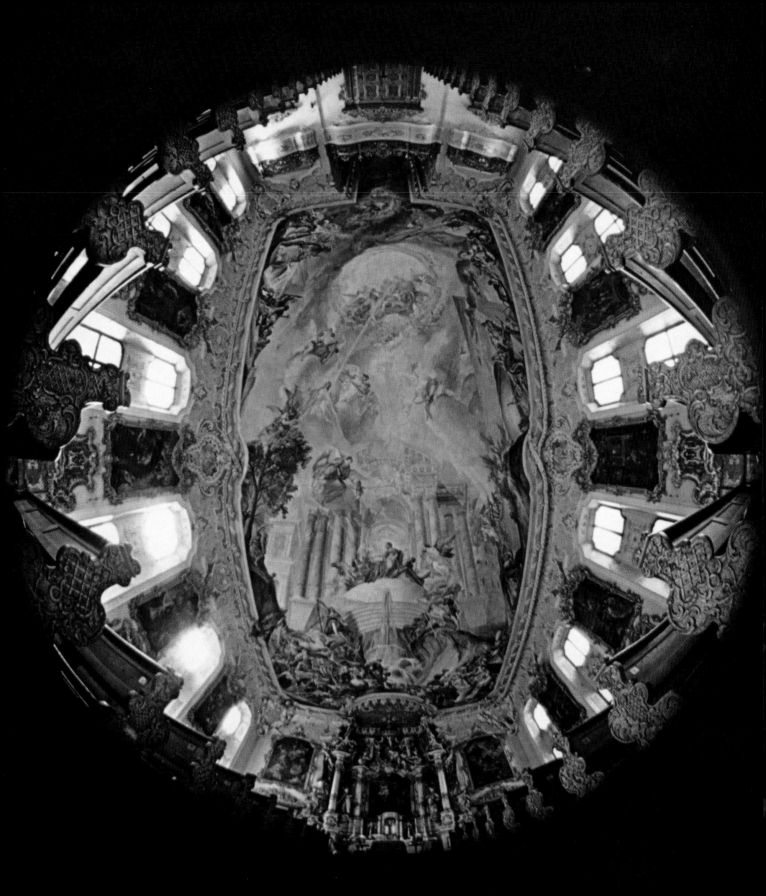

Europe, built his Hall of Liberation on a high hill outside Kelheim. The building is a pompous nightmare, filled with marble columns and statues representing German military victories, but its highest gallery affords a glorious panorama of the Danube valley. On the horizon one sees the walls and towers of ancient Regensburg; it is there that the Danube reaches its northernmost point and the summit of its early career.

The Celts, first to put down roots at the confluence of the Danube and the much smaller Regen, called their settlement Ratisbona. The Romans first camped in the area in A.D. 77; by A.D. 179 they had built a military fortress next to the Celtic town, calling it Castra Regina. Strategically located on the river, the outpost served the Romans as a center of trade as well as a home port for their Danube flotilla.

In the sixth century, the dukes of Bavaria set up residence in a fortress built upon the foundation of the Roman Porta Praetoria, the north gate of

At Kelheim, thirty miles downriver from Ingolstadt, the Danube acquires another major tributary, one that links the upper river to Western Europe's inland waterway system. The Danube is now a full-fledged commercial artery, carrying a steady flow of produce (including such mundane items as the milk cans seen at near right) and requiring steady maintenance (above). From the Hall of Liberation (opposite, above), an ersatz Valhalla overlooking Kelheim, it is possible to see for miles down the heavily settled basin (opposite, below).

the legionnaires' citadel, and the city was given its present name. In 1245 Regensburg became a free city of the Holy Roman Empire, and for two centuries it remained the wealthiest trading city in southern Germany. Regensburg's most famous landmark is the Steinerne Brücke, the Romanesque stone bridge linking the medieval town with Stadtamhof across the Danube. Construction began in 1135 and lasted eleven years; after eight hundred years the bridge remains an engineering miracle. Made of large squares of hewn stone, it is not so much a bridge as a stone wall thrown across the Danube. This most famous of all Danube bridges is 1,150 feet long, its fifteen long arches resting on piles of oak. Over the centuries hostile armies often tried to destroy Regensburg's stone bridge, and in 1945 the Americans did succeed in blowing up two arches. Now fully restored, the glorious bridge gives the medieval town its special character.

From 1663 to 1806, Regensburg's Town Hall was the seat of the first all-

Regensburg, one of the oldest settlements in the Danube valley, lies at the northern apex of the river's course. The city's first inhabitants were Celts, but its oldest structure, the 1,800-year-old Porta Praetoria (right), is Roman. The Old Stone Bridge (below), the first permanent span across the Danube, was completed in 1146, a century before Regensburg became a free city within the Holy Roman Empire. This river entrepôt was also the home of Germany's first parliament, which convened above the torture chamber seen at lower right.

German parliament, "the perpetual Diet," which was not dismissed until the collapse of the Holy Roman Empire. Conquered by Napoleon in 1809, Regensburg was demoted to the status of provincial capital of Bavaria. Johannes Kepler, the great astronomer who advised the noted Austrian general Albrecht von Wallenstein, died in Regensburg in 1630.

The next important point on the German Danube is Straubing, remembered for Agnes Bernauer. Young Albert of Bavaria fell in love with Agnes, "a beautiful and virtuous commoner" from Augsburg, secretly married her, and lived with her, ecstatically, at his castles in Vohburg and Straubing. Alas, Albert's father, the ruling Duke Ernest, had other plans for his son, and while Albert was away on official business Agnes was arrested for sorcery, brought before the ducal judges, and sentenced to death for having "bewitched" her husband. Poor Agnes was taken to the Danube and thrown into the water. She managed to reach the riverbank, but one of the duke's men "caught her long hair with a hooked pole and held her head under water until she was dead." A judge reported to the duke that "the Bernauerin has been dispatched to Heaven."

The lovely countryside has other sinister memories. In Deggendorf, a village built on a granite promontory, the people were said to live so sinfully that even the devil's ire was at last aroused. He brought an enormous stone

The bucolic serenity of the last leg of the German Danube (above) belies the region's troubled history. A poignant chapter in that chronicle was written in 1435 when Agnes Bernauer, the commoner wife of a young Bavarian prince, was adjudged guilty of witchcraft and drowned in the Danube. Her mortal remains are preserved today in a sarcophagus (above, right) at Straubing; her unhappy fate, in legend and song.

all the way from Italy, intending to drop it on the village. But when he heard the sweet bells of the monastery church, he dropped the stone on the southern side of the river—where it can still be seen. Deggendorf seems to have remained under the influence of the devil: one day in 1337 all the Jews of the village were massacred "because it was whispered that one of them had stolen a consecrated wafer." The chronicler adds that "most people in the village had been heavily in debt to the Jews. . . ."

After thirty more miles of charming countryside the Danube reaches the medieval city of Passau, located at the confluence of the small Ilz and the Inn with the Danube. The Inn, actually wider than the Danube at this point, flows parallel to it for a while, as though unable to decide whether or not to become a tributary. The Inn's depth, however, is only eight feet; the Danube's, twice as much. The confluence of three rivers can be a particularly dangerous spot, as the unsuspecting citizens of Passau learned on July 9, 1954, when the Danube reached an all-time level of 39.2 feet and, within a few hours, flooded the city completely. On the square in front of the Rathaus, the waters actually rose high enough to touch the tip of the nose of the statue of Empress Elizabeth.

Passau, the last city on the German Danube, perfectly sums up the river's youth. Like Regensburg, it was first a Celtic settlement and later a Roman command post. In the sixth century it became a bastion of Bavar-

The village of Deggendorf (above), twenty miles below Straubing, lies in the shadow of Devil's Rock, a heavily forested outcrop (visible at center rear) that was supposedly deposited there in the Middle Ages by Satan himself.

OVERLEAF: *The storybook city of Passau straddles the confluence of the Inn (foreground) and the narrower but far deeper Danube (middleground). Here the river finally sheds the last traces of its youth and flows into Austria.*

ian Catholicism. For centuries the bishops of Passau had greater power than the dukes and kings of Bavaria. They built Passau's beautiful cathedral, in which the Italian architect Rocco Lurago wed the older Gothic style with the younger baroque. The cathedral has the world's largest organ: 17,000 pipes, 211 stops, and a dynamic range from an almost inaudible *pianissimo* to an overpowering *fortissimo* that sounds like half a dozen large symphony orchestras performing simultaneously.

During the second Turkish siege of Vienna, in 1683, the Habsburg emperor Leopold I retreated to Passau, where plans were made for breaking the siege. On September 12, 1683, thirty-three princes and generals heard mass at Leopoldsberg Castle overlooking Vienna, and then at dawn the duke of Lorraine, supreme commander, gave the sign to attack. What followed was not a coordinated action but a series of minor encounters, and it confused and bewildered the exhausted defenders of Vienna. Around noon, there was a short pause while the duke held a command meeting. The Saxon General Goltz said, "I am an old man, I want comfortable quarters in Vienna tonight." King John III Sobieski of Poland agreed, and the final attack began at twenty minutes past three, "in the fierce heat of the afternoon." By four o'clock the Turks were in full flight. At 5:35, trumpets at Vienna's Schottentor announced the arrival of the first units of the relieving army; Vienna and Western civilization had been saved.

2

Blue Water, White Field

*M*en and women have lived in the Danube Basin since the dawn of history, but so little is known of the region's earliest settlers that archaeological speculation about them often fades into vague hypothesis. Human bones found in caves thirty miles southeast of Vienna, in the province of Burgenland, date from about 50,000 to 20,000 B.C., during the Paleolithic period. The oldest known relic, the Venus of Willendorf, named after the village on the Danube where it was found in 1908, is a small stone figure of a woman with a great protruding belly. Possibly a fertility symbol—and dating from around 20,000 B.C.—the Venus was created by people who were a cross between the Neanderthal and Cro-Magnon types.

The Danube Basin, by its narrowest geographical definition, is a thirty-mile-broad valley between the Alps and the Carpathians, Central Europe's major mountain ranges. Used as a geopolitical term, the basin includes such lands as Bohemia and southern Poland, which are far from the banks of the Danube but which have often come under its influence. The region's early history is obscure. There is a legend that some Trojans left Aeneas' band and reached the lower Danube in the fourteenth century B.C., but it has never been proved. The first peoples known to have lived in the basin were the Thracians and Thraco-Illyrians, who were probably attracted there from the Balkans and the Alps by the salt mines of Hallstatt, which thus has the distinction of being Austria's oldest community. The Hallstatt period, around 1000 B.C., was the first golden age of the Danube Basin; lasting perhaps five centuries, it was a peaceful era marked by the mining of salt, copper, iron, and gold.

The belligerent Celts changed all that when they arrived from the Swiss Alps and the plains of southern Germany in about 400 B.C. and proceeded along the Danube toward the Balkans, chasing the Thraco-Illyrians into the valleys of the Alps. One of several kingdoms the Celts established was Noricum, today's Lower Austria and Styria. Herodotus writes of a river called Istrols that was said to run through the land of the Celts. It must have been the Danube, for the river became a prominent symbol in Celtic myths and sagas; the Celts worshiped it as the greatest river they knew.

In the first century before the Christian Era, the Romans arrived from Italy, crossing the Alps and occupying what is now the Tyrol, Salzburg, Styria, Carinthia, and Upper and Lower Austria. Later the momentum of the Roman legions carried them farther east, into the plains of Hungary. They moved along the Danube, always along the river, and they left their imprint wherever they went. They called the region Pannonia and in 26 B.C. founded Carnuntum, their first settlement near the Danube, twenty-nine miles east of modern Vienna on a highway leading to what is now Bratislava, Czechoslovakia.

Strategically located in the narrow gap between the Alps and the Carpathians, Carnuntum became the first fortified Roman town in the Danube Basin, an administrative center and the perfect base for military expeditions. In the second century of the Christian Era, Carnuntum was a northern capital and occasional residence of the Roman emperors, whose rule extended from Egypt to Britannia and encompassed almost 15 percent of the then-known world. With its thick walls, great temples, and amphitheater seating 13,000 spectators, Carnuntum reflected Roman might. And in the nearby spa of Baden, sybaritic Romans could attempt to cure their gout in hot sulphur springs.

The earliest mention of what is today's Vienna can be found in Pliny the Elder's book *Natural History*, written in A.D. 77. Pliny mentions Vianiomina, the garrison of the Roman Thirteenth Legion, which had been visited sixty-eight years earlier by Tiberius Claudius Nero. Local historians now claim it was the young wives of Vianiomina that tempted the Romans to stay there. The vineyards themselves antedated the arrival of the Romans, but only around A.D. 276 did the Emperor Probus, now widely revered by the vintners of the world, tell the natives how to make decent wines. (Probus was not from Rome but was a native son, from Sirmium.) Wine-making retained its importance in the Danube Basin. In 1524 Archduke Ferdinard, who became Emperor Ferdinand I, called wine "the principal nourishment of the city of Vienna," and all Austrian sovereigns considered wines a prime source of taxation. Imports from elsewhere were restricted and for centuries the brewing of beer was prohibited.

The Romans brought civilization and laws to the region. They taught the native Celts not only to cultivate the soil and make good wine but to build roads and baths and to fortify the town soon called Vindobona, from the Celtic words *vindo* ("white") and *bona* ("field"). When the Roman soldiers and officials in the capital of Carnuntum wanted to relax, they went to Vindobona, where wine, women, and song were more abundant. Among the inhabitants of ancient Vindobona were Romans, Pannonians, Noricans from Noricum, Marcomanni from Bohemia, the Germanic Quadi, and quite a few Syrians, Egyptians, and Jews from the Roman colonies. Gradually, the legionnaires turned the garrison into a fortress. The inner city became a castle with thick walls, towers, and gates. In its center stood the praetorium, the offices of the commanders, and the administrative buildings. From there the main streets radiated outward—toward temples, the present-day Kohlmarkt ("coal market"), and the Gothic church

The Danube Basin has supported human life since the Paleolithic age. Not until 20,000 B.C., however, did it produce a vigorous indigenous culture—and with it the so-called Willendorf Venus (above). This squat and rotund figurine—the basin's oldest artifact—takes its name from the Danubian hamlet where it was found in 1908.

The handiwork of ancient Rome's vaunted engineers survives (above), but all else has vanished from Carnuntum, the first fortified Roman outpost in the Danube Basin. Carnuntum served for a time as the empire's northern capital, but it was the nearby garrison town of Vindobona that grew and prospered. By A.D. 171 this heavily fortified town—known today as Vienna—had become the bulwark of Rome's German empire.

of Maria am Gestade ("Mary by the Waterside"), built by fishermen—toward the banks of the Danube itself, where the military city ended. Inundated countless times over the next two millennia, the citizens of Vienna accepted periodic flooding as a fact of life. Then, in the 1870s, the course of the river was diverted north of the city. As a result, Vienna is no longer located directly on the Danube, and the Roman Danube has become the Danube Canal.

Trajan, who became emperor in A.D. 98, replaced the Thirteenth Legion with his personal favorite, the Tenth Legion, which remained in Vienna until the end of Roman rule. The soldiers of the Tenth Legion were a dashing, cosmopolitan group from many parts of the Western world. Gradually, however, they were conquered by the *genius loci* of the city—a phenomenon that affected many later conquerors as well. In the year 171, Emperor Marcus Aurelius ordered the Tenth Legion to attack the wild Germanic tribes that had approached from the east and were terrorizing the countryside, making sudden hit-and-run raids. The military campaign lasted longer than expected and created grave supply problems. Many civilians had taken refuge in the fortified part of Vindobona, and there was a critical shortage of drinking water that ended only after a "miraculous" cloudburst. The miracle occurred just in time, as we know from Marcus Aurelius's victory column in Rome with reliefs showing the emperor crossing the Danube, the river god Danubius, and Pluvius, the god of rain, with water pouring down his hair and from his outstretched arms.

Marcus Aurelius was in many ways a very unusual ruler. When, for example, Ariogaesus, prince of the Quadi and leader of the defeated Germanic tribes, was brought to the praetorium to be executed, as was then the Roman custom, the emperor decreed that the prince be exiled instead. The hostile tribes were also leniently treated, but they had to cede a strip of land four-and-a-half miles wide on the left bank of the Danube, where the Romans built fortifications to protect the northern approach to Vindobona. Marcus Aurelius, statesman and philosopher, then began to write his *Meditations*, which is now considered the first major literary work created in the city of Vienna.

Before long, however, other barbarian tribes from the north and east were creating havoc in the Roman provinces. Watching the destruction from the walls of Vindobona and Carnuntum, Marcus Aurelius reluctantly gave orders to start another campaign. Early in March of 180, when the ice had disappeared from the Danube, Roman engineers built pontoon bridges across the river. It was rumored in town that the emperor himself, in full battle regalia, would cross the Danube and lead his troops into battle. Eager to witness this great spectacle, the inhabitants of Vindobona gathered by the river, waiting and watching. But Marcus Aurelius did not appear, and on March 17 it was announced that he had died and would be succeeded by his son Commodus.

The old emperor had been able to complete his *Meditations* on Stoicism before dying, but few people would read his work, which had been written in Greek, the language of scholars and intellectuals. He had left orders that his trusted general, Claudius Pompejanus, should lead the campaign against the Germanic tribes. But Emperor Commodus was no statesman; he was utterly unconcerned about the fate of Rome's eastern provinces and wanted nothing so much as to return to Rome's *dolce vita*. As a result, Pompejanus was told to carry out only absolutely necessary operations. Soon negotiations got under way, with Commodus promising no further annexation of enemy lands beyond the narrow strip north of the Danube and refusing the advice of his generals, who said that such concessions were bound to encourage the aggressors. Marcus Aurelius had forbidden the formation of national assemblies by the tribes because such meetings might create trouble. Commodus revoked his father's ban; henceforth assemblies would be permitted if they were attended by a Roman officer. Inevitably these officers, who had to understand the language of the tribes and were often former tribesmen, soon became partisans of their kinsmen.

The Germanic tribes were quick to exploit the Romans' weakness after Commodus returned to Rome, and they soon ruled the north bank of the river. Fearing for their safety, many longtime residents of the Danube's nether bank left their homes and resettled closer to the Roman soldiers, who still kept a semblance of law and order south of the river. But among the new immigrants were fifth columnists, and morale soon broke down in both Carnuntum and Vindobona. Emperor Commodus never bothered to return to Pannonia, dying in Rome in 192 at the age of thirty-two, and the following year the legionnaires in Carnuntum elected their garrison commander, Septimius Severus, emperor; he soon seized Rome. It was a great day for Carnuntum, and there was much jealous muttering in Vindobona. An African-born professional soldier who had style and charisma, Septimius was followed in 211 by his son Caracalla, who honored Vindobona by

It was from Vindobona, not Carnuntum, that Marcus Aurelius orchestrated his campaign against the Germanic tribes, and it was there that his troops sought refuge when the tide of battle turned against them. A panel from the emperor's victory column in Rome (directly below) shows Pluvius, the god of rain, shedding his welcome waters upon the thirsty citizens of the beleaguered city. A second panel (below, left) depicts the emperor crossing a pontoon bridge over the Danube at the head of an avenging army.

By A.D. 303 *the once peaceful Roman Empire had been engulfed by rebellion. Emperor Diocletian, who blamed this turmoil on the Christians, initiated a systematic empirewide purge of the young sect.. One of the first victims of these persecutions was Florian, patron saint of Upper Austria. Albrecht Altdorfer's version of* The Martyrdom of Saint Florian *(right) shows the pious cleric being clubbed to death. Other sources suggest that he may have been drowned in the Danube instead.*

making it a *municipium*, the only Danubian city to hold that rank, with two *duumviri*, or co-mayors, who were to control one another.

In A.D. 249, Vindobona was given a patron goddess, Fortuna Conservatrix. The choice was an auspicious one, for over the years the city was to endure an incredible succession of disasters—fires, plagues, wars, sieges—that might have swept the settlement off the map, had Fortuna not always been on the side of the inhabitants. During this same period the Romans also built a harbor at Vindobona, an artificial basin 750 feet long, 230 feet wide, and surrounded by dams and moles. This was to be the home port of the Romans' mighty Danube flotilla, a two-hundred-ship armada that patrolled the river all the way to the delta. The Romans hoped the mere presence of their ships would be an effective deterrent to barbarian incursions.

By the year 300 Christianity was beginning to spread among the citizens of Vindobona, but this in no way altered their studied indifference to the Roman pagans, who continued to build temples to their gods, among them Danubius and Agaunus, the patron of the Wien, a small Danube tributary that flows through the town and that later gave Vienna its name. In 270 Emperor Aurelianus, another professional soldier, came out from Rome in an attempt to save the crumbling empire. He managed to stop the invasion of the Goths, but the citizens of Vindobona hardly cared; they had already acquired political sophistication, contempt for military power, and a great interest in spectacles and music. When Emperor Probus surrounded himself with the Batavi, an elite guard of hulking, noisy, uncouth men from the region now known as the Netherlands, men who could be very dangerous when they got drunk, the Vindobonians carefully avoided them. And no one was particularly upset when Probus was killed during a mutiny staged by besotted Batavian soldiers.

Emperor Diocletian, a native of Dalmatia and the eventual successor to Probus, put down a series of rebellions inside his empire, in the course of which he became convinced that he was the victim of a Christian conspiracy. He therefore initiated a large-scale persecution of Christians and, in the process, gave the inhabitants of the Danube Basin their first martyr-saint, Florian, who refused to give up his faith and was either buried alive or drowned in the Danube as a result. (The site of Saint Florian's tomb, located in a beautiful baroque monastery near the confluence of the Enns and the Danube, is also noteworthy because Anton Bruckner, the great nineteenth-century composer, was organist there and is buried on the grounds.) The savage persecutions ordered by Diocletian continued for nearly a decade after his retirement, ending in 313, the year of his death, when Emperor Constantine decreed tolerance toward the Christians in his historic Edict of Milan. Constantine then undertook a lengthy royal progress aimed at selecting a new imperial capital, visiting Carnuntum and Vindobona, among other cities, before eventually selecting Byzantium. As Christianity spread along the Danube, temples were gradually converted into churches, but there was no religious fanaticism. The Danubians had already learned to live and let live, always following the line of least resistance. Indeed, resistance was hardly necessary, for the Roman Empire was quite clearly in decline.

During the fourth century Rome's eastern provinces were overrun by successive waves of savage barbarians. First there were the Visigoths (western Goths), from the lower Danube, and the Ostrogoths (eastern Goths), who had lived along the river Don. These peoples reached the Danube Basin not as invaders but as fugitives, running before the seemingly invincible Huns, who had come out of Siberia, spreading terror throughout Europe when they appeared in 370. The Huns were swarthy, short, black-haired nomads, "unwashed and badly smelling." To the early Christians they were nothing less than the Horsemen of the Apocalypse. Whole tribes fled before them toward the Roman provinces, where they hoped to find safety.

In 395, some 12,000 Visigoths under a chieftain named Alaric crossed the frozen Danube and invaded Dacia, now roughly modern Romania. Consolidating his army and continuing toward the Balkans, Alaric conquered a number of Roman garrisons located along the lower stretches of the Danube and in northern Greece.

Four years after Alaric's initial incursion, Rome made a desperate effort to reverse the barbarian tide. It was proclaimed, according to author Erwin Lessner, that "All Romans must defend their state. . . . The barbarians must be given the choice of either returning beyond the Danube and telling their kin that they are unwanted in Rome and Byzantium, or to stay here as bondsmen and till the soil for the benefit of their Roman masters." The threat was a hollow one, however, for the once omnipotent Roman masters had no way of enforcing their decree, which was simply ignored by the approaching Huns. Some Roman commanders tried to make deals with

The Danube has always been a two-way highway of conquest. During the first century of the Christian era the Romans established a flotilla at Vindobona—and then gradually extended their rule to the east. Two hundred years later a Visigoth army reversed the process: securing a foothold in what is today Romania, the barbarians swept upriver as far as Vindobona itself. Their leader's name was Alaric, and it is his deceptively benign features that grace the signet ring seen above.

Significantly, the Visigoths entered the Danube Basin out of necessity, not lust for conquest. Driven from their homelands and pursued westward by the awesome Huns, Alaric's followers had sought sanctuary beyond the Carpathian Alps. That divide proved no obstacle for the swarthy horsemen of inner Asia —one of whom is featured on the funeral stele above—and the Huns soon overran the upper valley (right).

the illiterate horsemen, hoping to enlist them as auxiliaries or use them for their own ambitious schemes. It was too late; the Huns could not be stopped. "The Huns appear when they are least expected," wrote a gravely troubled Saint Eusebius Hieronymus from Pannonia. "They do not respect religion, age or station, they won't even spare helpless children. . . . Roman blood is spilled every day . . . lands are overrun and ravaged . . . . Cruel despair spreads everywhere. . . ."

Darkness settled over the Danube Basin as, for almost a century, the Huns overran the area. In 487 the legionnaires were finally ordered to return to Rome, and nearly five centuries of Roman rule came to an end. Attila, king of the Huns, ruled Eastern and Central Europe from the delta to the Danube to Vindobona, until his death in 453. His was a monstrous regime despite the fact that some German historians consider him an honorary Goth and others speculate that he may be King Etzel of the *Nibelungenlied*, the heroic German folk saga of the Danube.

After the departure of the Romans, the recorded history of the Danube Basin is sketchy and confusing. The name of Vindobona appears in the old records until the end of the fifth century. Without protection by the Romans, the town became unsafe and was probably deserted by its inhabitants. Then there were almost five hundred years of silence before "Wiennis" (Wien) was mentioned in the Niederaltaich Annals of 1030.

Even a cursory review of these unknown centuries conveys a frightening picture, for the migration of nomadic tribes from the east continued through the Danube Basin. The Huns retreated in the latter half of the fifth century, but at the turn of the sixth century the Avars arrived in the region—and history repeated itself. They too came from Siberia, but they were of Turkish stock; though hardly civilized, they were not as brutal as the Huns. They subjugated some Slav tribes who were to survive their masters and found the state of Bulgaria in 680. The Langobards also reached the Danube, only to continue south toward Italy—where, as the Lombards, they were defeated by Charlemagne in 774.

Few facts and many legends exist about this great Christianizer and mysterious despot, but none doubt that Charlemagne also subdued the Avars, whose citadel was probably near Györ on the Danube, halfway between Budapest and Vienna. It was Charlemagne, too, who definitively and often forcefully established Christianity in the Danube Basin, although the new religion had for some time been spreading into the region from Rome in the south as well as from Constantinople in the east.

Among scholars, Charlemagne remains a subject of controversy, though all concede he was a great empire builder. In Rome, on Christmas Day of the year 800, he was crowned the first Holy Roman emperor by Pope Leo III. And at the time of his death, fourteen years later, his vast empire reached from Scandinavia to Spain, from the Atlantic to the Elbe. Although that empire was soon split up among his sons, Charlemagne's influence remained. A farsighted man, he had established small buffer states in the regions once ruled by the Romans and had obliged their rulers to swear allegiance to him in the imperial residence at Ratisbon, modern

Regensburg. One of these buffer states was the Ostmark, which is known today as Osterreich or Austria.

As Charlemagne's empire fell into disarray, other invading tribes poured into the Danube Basin. From the west came the Franks and Bajuvars, predecessors of today's Bavarians; from the east, the Magyars. These last were, according to a biased and imaginative ninth-century chronicler, "of sickening ugliness. . . . Their voices were frighteningly shrill, and their language was different from any other human tongue. Like wild animals, they devoured raw flesh and drank blood." Like the Huns, to whom they were often unfairly compared, the Magyars came from the mysterious reaches of Siberia, the cradle of many nations. By the end of the century, one of their chieftains, Prince Arpád, had reached the Danube and established his residence on an island in the river. He called the site Csepel; today it is the main industrial district of the Hungarian capital of Budapest.

The Magyars had always been soldiers, people who believed that life was not to be lived but to be fought. From Hungary they invaded Lower Austria, Upper Austria, Carinthia, and Italy. Eventually they dominated the Danube valley as far west as Ratisbon. Occasionally local princes and bishops rallied against the Magyars, and on one occasion the soldiers of Richarius, Bishop of Passau, killed twelve hundred of them near the Abbey of

Saint Florian. Eventually the Magyars met their fate on the Lechfeld, near Augsburg, Germany, twenty-five miles south of the Danube, where they were brutally annihilated in August, 955, by the Christian soldiers of King Otto I of Germany. This historical battle drew a line between Eastern and Western Europe, one that was to endure for almost a thousand years, until the end of World War II.

Seven years later, Otto was crowned Holy Roman Emperor. And in 975 his son, Otto II, established diplomatic relations with the Magyars, who were being converted to Christianity. The real power of the Magyar court at Csepel was the legendary beauty Sarolta, wife of the ruler Géza. And it was her son Vaik, baptized in 994 and given the name Stephen, who became the founder and first king of modern Hungary.

Stephen's marriage at Ratisbon to Gisela, the sister of Emperor Otto III, was the social event of the decade, and their formal marriage contract served as the blueprint for Hungary's constitution and social system. (The royal couple's honeymoon trip down the Danube led past the Lechfeld and the battlefield where the bridegroom's ancestors had been massacred, not exactly a tactful itinerary.) For two centuries after the marriage, poets and minnesingers wrote and sang about the glorious event, which became more

Led by Attila, whom all Europe called "the Scourge of God," the Huns pressed steadily westward, forcing the Romans to abandon one riverside stronghold after another. In 487 Vindobona fell to the Huns, and shortly thereafter the barbarians established a command post of their own, upriver at Melk. Today a vast, imposing Benedictine monastery (opposite) stands on that site. Once the official residence of the Babenbergs, Austria's first hereditary sovereigns, this great abbey is known today for its magnificently frescoed ceiling (above).

glamorous with each poem. Some say Gisela is the "Burgundian princess" of the *Nibelungenlied* and Stephen, King Etzel.

The actual coronation of Stephen as king of Hungary had to be delayed temporarily because the Magyars in Csepel had no crown. To remedy this situation, Pope Sylvester II ordered his Roman jewelers to make a crown and also an apostolic cross, which was to be carried in front of the converted monarch during the ceremony. Otto III contributed a holy lance adorned with the relic of Saint Maurice, and the Church in Byzantium sent a crown of its own, hoping to neutralize Rome's influence in Hungary. A German artisan living in Csepel welded these two crowns into the Crown of Saint Stephen, and the much delayed coronation finally took place on Christmas Day in the year 1000 at Esztergom, which became the seat of Hungary's Catholic primate.

King Stephen died in 1038, and in 1087 he was canonized. Although he is not often mentioned in modern Hungarian history books, he remains alive in the hearts of the people. The Crown of Saint Stephen, which became a religious as well as a political symbol in Hungary, was brought out of the country at the end of World War II. Saved from Hungary's Nazi occupiers and also from its Soviet conquerors, it rests in a vault in Washington, D.C.—a fact that still acerbates relations between the United States and the Hungarian People's Republic.

Buda, a former Roman settlement, and its twin city on the left bank of the Danube, Pest, continued to grow in the twelfth century. Many Germans, Walloons, French, and Italians made the two towns important trade centers. Then once again savage invaders from Asia threatened the country's existence. After overrunning Russia and the lower Danube region, the armies of the Mongolian Great Khan Ogadai, son of Genghis Khan, appeared. The terrifying Mongolian horsemen were short and bowlegged, with black hair and prominent jawbones. They burned and looted Pest in the spring of 1241, killing the men, raping the women, and throwing the dead into the Danube. King Béla took refuge at the seaport of Spalatum in what is now Yugoslavia. Early the next year the Mongolians suddenly withdrew to their capital, Karakorum, six thousand miles away, because of the death of the Great Khan. (During the Hungarian Revolution of 1956 the Soviets sent Mongolian army units to Budapest, a gesture that shocked and frightened the Hungarians, who, even after seven hundred years, were still terrified of Mongolians.)

Five years after the unexpected departure of the invaders, King Béla ordered a network of fortresses built throughout the country. The stone fortress on the hill of Buda, overlooking the Danube, was completed in 1255, and at that time Buda was granted the status of an independent town. Later, this fortress became the royal residence and the site of the Roman settlement was renamed Obuda (old Buda). In 1286 the first Diet, an assembly of Hungarian noblemen, was held near the fortress, and it is said King Béla's daughter lived just below on an island in the Danube that still bears her name—Margaret Island.

After its destruction following the departure of the Romans and after

For the hapless residents of the Danube Basin, the Dark Ages were gloomy indeed: no sooner had the Huns withdrawn than the Avars appeared in their stead—only to give way to another barbarian band from inner Asia, the Magyars. These last were defeated in 955 at the Lechfeld, some twenty-five miles south of the Danube, in what was perhaps the most crucial battle of the Middle Ages. Otto I of Germany—who offers a church to Christ on the ivory bas-relief seen below—engineered that victory, which established a line of demarcation between East and West that lasted for a thousand years.

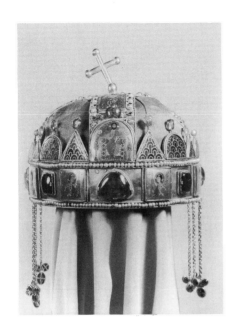

Outnumbered and outfought at the Lechfeld, the dispirited Magyars and their leader, Géza, retreated downriver to Csepel, an island fortress that later became the center of Budapest. There, in the year of the millennium, Géza's son Stephen was named Hungary's first king. Both the pope in Rome and the church in Byzantium supplied crowns for the ceremony, and these were welded into the distinctive Crown of Saint Stephen (above).

OVERLEAF: *Between Melk and Vienna the Danube passes through the castle-studded valley of the Wachau, where legend lies as thick as morning mist. It is said of one owner of Aggstein Castle (left, foreground) that he customarily offered captured enemies the option of starving to death in his keep or jumping to certain death in the gorge below.*

five centuries of neglect, Vienna was at last rebuilt in 1137, probably under Margrave Adalbert of Babenberg. The Babenbergs, who ruled the Ostmark after 976, were not native Austrians, but then none of Austria's ruling dynasties were native born. Instead, they were descended from a Franconian family named Bamberg that had supported the German emperors and been rewarded for its loyalty with possession of the Ostmark.

During the tenth and eleventh centuries the Ostmark enjoyed great prosperity, owing to fishing, gold washing, and trading along the Danube, salt-mining in Hallstatt, and wine-making around Vienna. As a result, the *civitas* of Vienna was granted special commercial privileges after 1137, and during the regime of Heinrich Jasomirgott (so named because he liked to say, *"Ja, so mir Gott helfe"*—"Yes, with God's help") Austria became a duchy and Vienna the residence of its rulers. The Babenbergs governed Austria for three centuries, and during that time two became sons-in-law of the emperors of Byzantium—yet another example of marriage as a valued instrument of Austrian power politics. During these years life was pleasant in Vienna, a prosperous trading center where Crusaders bound for the Holy Land could pause for diversions and buy provisions. Clearly the Viennese had already developed their philosophy of "let's be merry for tomorrow we die," which has served them admirably to this day.

Duke Leopold V of Babenberg is known outside of Austria because he quarreled with England's Richard the Lion-Hearted (third son of Henry II and Eleanor of Aquitaine), who was returning from a Crusade. Leopold had Richard arrested in 1192 and then held Richard for ransom for two years in Castle Dürnstein, a brooding fortress overlooking the Danube from the lovely Wachau hills, seventy miles upriver from Vienna.

The death of the last male Babenberg in 1246 was followed by an interregnum, years of terror that were consumed by arguments over the succession—arguments involving the pope, Emperor Frederick II, and various Austrian nobles. Four years later the emperor died, and with his death the House of Hohenstaufen was extinguished. The empire was in a state of chaos when Přemysl Ottokar, king of Bohemia, took over Vienna in 1251. Later Ottokar was to take over Austria, defeating King Béla of Hungary, who wanted to rule in Vienna himself.

Přemysl Ottokar, young and handsome, soon won the hearts of the Viennese by staging extravagant public festivities and patronizing poets and minnesingers, among them Tannhäuser from Salzburg (later immortalized in Richard Wagner's opera). "If you have got plenty of gold and silver, this is the place to spend it, to make merry, sing, revel," a thirteenth-century visitor to Vienna accurately and cheerfully reported. In 1252 Ottokar married Margaretha Babenberg. He was twenty-three; she was forty-six but very rich, and Ottokar needed money for his campaign against King Béla of Hungary. Their conflict was finally resolved through the forceful intervention of Pope Innocent IV, who in 1254 persuaded the two antagonists to meet at the castle in Pressburg, on a hill overlooking the Danube. Here it was determined that Ottokar should keep Austria, promising later to marry Cunigunde von Machow, the young and beautiful granddaughter of King

Equally skilled at battlefield strategy and international diplomacy, Rudolph of Habsburg secured the heart of what was to become the most famous of all Danube empires. Vienna was its capital, and it is there that Rudolph's likeness is preserved today in brilliant stained glass.

Béla. No one was apparently much bothered by the fact that Ottokar was still married. It did take seven years to have this first marriage annulled, however, and not until 1262 was Ottokar finally free to wed Cunigunde. At their wedding banquet, it was written, "the tables were so long you could walk between them for hours."

King Ottokar certainly knew the Viennese. When one tenth of the city burned down in 1258 he had churches and convents rebuilt at his expense and donated "a whole forest of timber" for new houses. A contemporary chronicler writes that noblemen and well-heeled travelers "stayed much longer in Vienna than their affairs demanded," and some lived so well that they eventually went bankrupt. Ottokar tried to consolidate and centralize his regime by abolishing the power of local rulers. He ordered many Austrian castles pulled down, and the noble ruins of the region, once thought to have been destroyed by invaders, are actually the handiwork of Ottokar's skilled wrecking squads. The young king also spoke of abolishing the Holy Roman Empire and replacing it by an alliance of strong European powers, with himself as *primus inter pares*—a radically modern concept centuries ahead of its time.

In 1273 the electors of Germany, gathered to select a new emperor, reached an impasse in their deliberations. To break this deadlock they finally settled upon an unknown compromise candidate, Rudolf, count of Habsburg, an impoverished nobleman from the Aargau region of Switzerland. His name derived from that of the ancestral castle, Habichtsburg ("hawk's nest")—often ridiculed as Habenichtsburg ("have-not castle"). An apprehensive Ottokar wrote to Pope Gregory X that he would never recognize Rudolf, whom he referred to as "that count who ought to carry a beggar's pouch and is hardly fit for any office."

For two years Rudolf and Ottokar played a fascinating game of international power politics, each trying to win away the other's supporters. Bribes were offered, pressure was exerted, informers were hired. Once again the Hungarians sought to interfere, siding with Rudolf despite the fact that Ottokar was married to King Béla's granddaughter. Ottokar, no longer safe in Vienna, returned to Prague—and Rudolf promptly declared "the ban of the Reich" against him. A Habsburg army marched down the Danube valley, which once again had become the road to war. Simultaneously, heavy siege equipment was loaded on low barges at Ratisbon and floated downriver toward Ottokar's abandoned capital. After occupying Passau and Linz, Rudolf at last turned his attention to Vienna. One by one, the local noblemen defected from Ottokar's ranks to join the invader, who at last reached the Wienerwald (Vienna Woods), the forest surrounding the city. Meanwhile Ottokar's army, much attenuated by defections, had regrouped at the Marchfeld, a large plain northeast of Vienna that is visible on a clear day from the hills of the Wienerwald.

Both leaders were reluctant to join battle, and Rudolf therefore offered Ottokar an "honorable" compromise, one that permitted him to keep Bohemia and Moravia—but as a Habsburg vassal. There would be peace between Bohemia and Hungary, a general amnesty, and no reprisals against the Viennese who had elected to remain loyal to Ottokar. Late in 1276, the two kings met on a meadow outside the city walls to sign the agreement. As the Viennese onlookers held their breath, King Ottokar knelt down before Rudolf to receive his investiture. Shortly thereafter, Ottokar returned to Prague to consolidate his forces and plot his revenge; as far as he was concerned, the war was only postponed. Meanwhile, in Vienna, Rudolf arranged to marry his daughter Clementine to Ladislas IV, the new king of Hungary. This deal was to pay off handsomely: when the inevitable confrontation with Ottokar came, Ladislas was to dispatch some 35,000 Hungarian soldiers to swell the ranks of the Habsburg army.

The battle of Marchfeld, as the critical confrontation is known, began on the morning of August 26, 1278. For several hours neither side gained an advantage, but when Ottokar's Bohemian forces launched a massive afternoon attack, Rudolf's troops suffered severe casualties. The emperor's own horse was killed, and Rudolf had to be rescued by one of the knights. At that point Ulrich von Kappel, a Styrian nobleman loyal to the emperor, led a paltry force of fifty armored horsemen in a suicidal countercharge. Miraculously, they succeeded in repelling the Bohemian attack, giving Rudolf's Hungarian allies time to enter the fray—and suddenly the Bohemian forces were routed. King Ottokar was jolted from his saddle by a lance, and his sword was torn from his hand. By the rules of chivalry, the dismounted and unarmed king should have been treated with the honor traditionally accorded royal prisoners. Instead, Berthold von Emerberg, one of Rudolf's retainers, stepped forth and dispatched Ottokar. Five hundred years later, the great Austrian playwright Franz Grillparzer was to write a controversial patriotic play, *König Ottokar's Glück und Ende* ("King Ottokar's Fortunes and Fall"), in which Rudolf renders homage to the killed foe. Actually, he did no such thing; his army and the Hungarians pursued the fleeing Bohemians mercilessly, killing at least ten thousand of them. The Hungarians, for their part, behaved so brutally toward the vanquished foe that Rudolf finally implored King Ladislas to take his wild men and go home.

The battle of Marchfeld, which assured the future of the Holy Roman Empire, also made Vienna the capital of the Habsburgs' Danube monarchy for 640 years. The dust of battle had hardly settled when Rudolf, in a display of the matchmaking zeal that was to characterize Habsburg dynasts, arranged two wound-binding political marriages: the first between his son Rudolf and Ottokar's daughter Agnes, the second between his daughter Judith and Ottokar's son Wenceslaus, who was then seven years old. Vienna remained the principal capital of the Habsburgs even when members of collateral branches of the family settled elsewhere. Curiously, Rudolf, the first Habsburg, has no statue in Vienna. When this was pointed out in 1914, a committee was set up and Archduke Francis Ferdinand attended a gala fund-raising party, but a few weeks later he was assassinated at Sarajevo, an event that signaled the beginning of the end for the Habsburgs. And thus Rudolf failed to get his statue—and it now seems highly unlikely that he ever will.

3
Storm Out of Asia

*T*he early fourteenth century brought a chain of disasters to the Danube Basin. In 1327 a considerable part of Vienna burned to the ground. Eleven years later, in June, clouds of locusts said to have come from Asia—as had earlier invaders—settled on the fields and destroyed the harvest. Ironically, only the Austrian vineyards resisted the locusts, and in the fall there was hunger and much drunkenness along the Danube because wine had become the only nourishment. The terrible locusts returned the following spring, and the resultant famine of 1339 killed more people than had the war between Rudolf and Ottokar.

No sooner had the locusts left than people living near the Danube were beset by repeated floods—which some said were ordered by an angry God to punish sinners. (It was widely held that the disasters had been caused by "resurrected demons.") Many villages along the river were literally swept away by the raging waters; the survivors promptly rebuilt their villages, exactly replicating what had been lost, as people are wont to do. In 1342 the floods returned, and these new houses were swept away too. The humbled citizenry then insisted that the world was coming to an end—as indeed it seemed to do on January 25, 1348, when a terrible earthquake shook the Danube Valley. Thousands died, and the town of Villach in Carinthia was reduced to rubble. Not surprisingly, the Jews were blamed for the disaster, although there were not many left in Austria after the pogroms of 1338.

Just as people began to forget the earthquake, the basin was struck by bubonic plague, called the Black Death, and between 1349 and 1713 at least fourteen major epidemics of the plague raged in Vienna. Tens of thousands died in Austria in 1349; in Vienna, five hundred people perished every day. At Saint Stephen's Cathedral alone, fifty-four clergymen died of the disease. It was said that only flagellation would soothe the demons, and processions of flagellants began appearing in towns and villages even though the Church forbade the pagan ceremonies.

As soon as the plague had run its course in Vienna, the city returned to its former ways. Under Duke Otto the Merry, a man who considered life a permanent festival, nobles wore cloaks edged with small silver bells. Even stern justice tried to show a merry face: petty criminals were ordered to sit in large dog kennels, where they were exposed to public ridicule, and dishonest bakers were put in a large cage that was slowly lowered into the Danube. When the Crusaders came through Vienna in May of 1395, they liked the city so much that they tarried for more than a year. As a result of their merrymaking, many historians believe, the Crusaders were disastrously beaten by the Turks near Nikopol late in 1396; thousands perished in the muddy waters of the Danube. Ominously, the Turks had gained a foothold in Europe.

The political situation along the Danube in the fourteenth century reflected the chaos created by successive natural disasters. Crowns were traded, countries were sold, rulers were killed, mercenaries were hired by pretenders, and intertwining marriages were created through intrigues. After the collapse of the Arpádian dynasty in 1301, Hungary was ruled successively by a Bohemian king, a Bavarian, members of the House of Anjou, and Sigismund of Brandenburg. The Bohemian king, Wenceslaus II, was married to a Habsburg and became the king of Poland, extending Habsburg suzerainty from the lower Rhine to the central Danube. In Bohemia the Premysls were succeeded by the House of Luxemburg and for some time the focus of European history shifted to Prague, which Goethe later called "a continent in the middle of a continent."

Much of Prague's Gothic beauty goes back to Charles IV, the great Luxemburger who became Holy Roman emperor in 1347 and helped found Prague University, the first in Central Europe, a year later. Its rector from 1402 to 1403 was Jan Hus, a lecturer, ordained priest, and popular preacher whose teachings became the focus of the later Hussite movement, a national revolution that was to sustain the identity of the nation for five hundred years. Originally, Hussitism was an intellectual movement, spurred by its leader's many close contacts with the universities of Paris and Oxford, especially with John Wycliffe who taught at Oxford. It soon developed social and religious overtones, however, as Hus inveighed against the excesses of the Catholic church. Too many starved while a few had too much, Hus insisted, adding that circumstances obliged him to doubt the infallibility of the pope. Told to recant, Hus refused. In 1414 he was summoned to the Council of Constance, where—in spite of an imperial promise of safe-conduct—he was thrown in prison. On June 6, 1415, he was burned at the stake as an "incorrigible heretic." His teachings could not be committed to the flames, however. Inspired by them, the peasantry rose up against the nobility in the Hussite wars from 1419 to 1434, and Hussitism became the forerunner of the Reformation.

In the middle of the fifteenth century Habsburg emperor Frederick III promoted all members of his house from duke to archduke and adopted as his motto A.E.I.O.U., which meant *Austriae Est Imperare Orbi Universo* (Austria shall rule the whole world) or *Austriae Erit In Orbe Ultima* (Austria will be the last on earth). This arrogant motto was widely ridiculed. It was also astonishingly prophetic, for Frederick's own son, Maximilian I, turned the motto into history. Maximilian was a brilliant boy and a tal-

Through a series of astute political marriages Habsburg emperor Maximilian I gave credence to his family's overweening motto: "Austria shall rule the whole world." The first of these marital alliances, made when Maximilian was only eighteen, added Burgundy and the Low Countries to his burgeoning realm. In this detail from Altdorfer's The Triumphal Procession of Maximilian I, *the Burgundian colors are trooped.*

ented linguist who spoke German, Latin, French, Italian, Spanish, English, Wendish, and Flemish. At eighteen, he obediently married Mary of Burgundy, thus adding the Burgundian possessions in France and the Low Countries to his realm. His military reforms abolished the armored cavalry and emphasized the importance of the infantry. He also introduced hand firearms and increased the firepower of the imperial army's artillery.

After the early death of his wife in 1482, Maximilian married Anne of Brittany—perhaps hoping to become king of France in the bargain—but the marriage was annulled. The emperor's frankly expansionist marriage policy was well summed up by King Matthias Corvinus Hunyadi of Hungary, who said, *"Bella gerant alii tu, felix Austria, nube!"*—"Let others wage war; you, lucky Austria, marry!" Maximilian was by then the acknowledged grand master of matrimonial politics. In 1496 he had his son Philip the Handsome married to Juana of Castile, daughter of Ferdinand and Isabella, thus establishing the Habsburg line in Spain.

An able practitioner of what he preached, Maximilian had taken a third wife, Bianca Maria Sforza of Milan, in 1494, giving the Habsburgs a secure foothold in Italy. And in 1515 he pulled off his greatest matrimonial coup with the astonishing Treaty of Vienna. Under its terms his grandson Ferdinand would marry Anna of Hungary and Bohemia, and his granddaughter Mary would marry Louis II, heir to the throne of Hungary. The Treaty of Vienna made Austria, Hungary, and Bohemia the central core of an expanded and vital Habsburg monarchy. In this instance the betrothed were all between nine and twelve years of age, but this did not deter the emperor—and when a Habsburg, even a child, was told to marry, he or she did his duty.

The double marriage ratifying the Treaty of Vienna took place on July 22, 1515, at Saint Stephen's Cathedral. Fine musical accompaniment was provided by the baroque *Hofmusikkapelle*, which Maximilian had established in 1496. This great orchestra had more than a hundred members, mostly Italians, and it enjoyed a yearly subsidy of some 60,000 florins. (Next to matrimony, music was the most important matter of state for the Habsburgs. Viennese historians claim that the *Hofmusikkapelle* was the predecessor of the Vienna Philharmonic, "the world's oldest orchestra.") While the musicians played inside the church, the military field bands of four nations, accompanied by two hundred trumpeters and drummers from the emperor's forces, performed in the streets, making "an ear-splitting noise." Chroniclers counted sixteen princes, three dukes, two cardinals, and fifteen bishops at the banquet tables. And when the festivities ended, Maximilian journeyed to Augsburg where he labored to convince the members of the Diet to elect his grandson Charles as Holy Roman emperor. The emperor died of a stroke in 1519, one year before Charles V was crowned in Aix-la-Chapelle. Charles was at the same time the king of Spain, Aragon, Sicily, and Naples. With some justification, he could claim to rule an empire "on which the sun never sets."

While the Habsburg empire increased by carefully planned marriages, a different sort of expansion took place in the Orient. There the sprawl-

On July 22, 1515, the great nave of Saint Stephen's Cathedral (opposite) reverberated with joyous sound. To celebrate the double wedding of two of his grandchildren—and through that happy event the final consolidation of the Austro-Hungarian Empire—Maximilian assembled the world's first major orchestra. Outside, beneath the church's gay mosaic roofs (above), some two hundred trumpeters and drummers broadcast the news of the emperor's triumph.

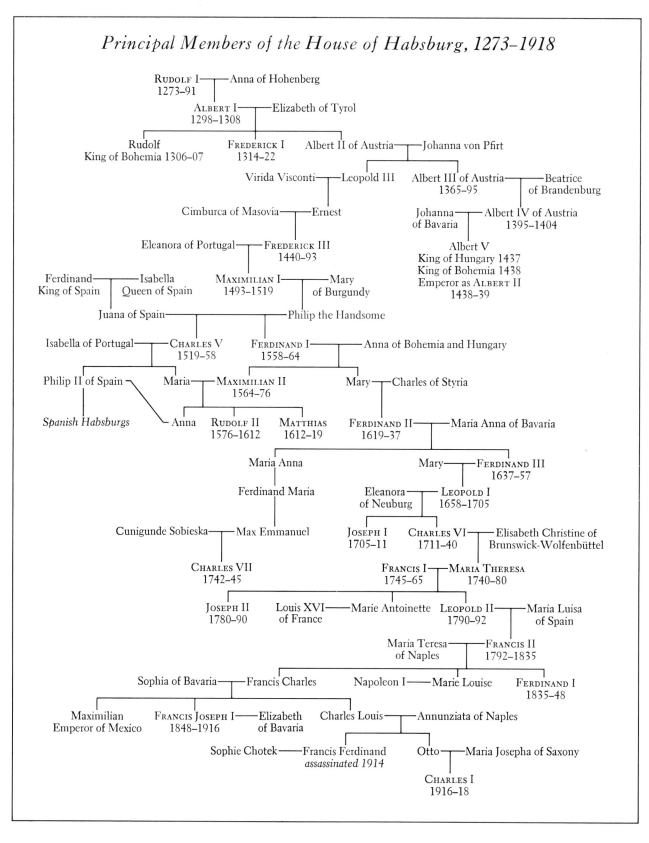

Principal Members of the House of Habsburg, 1273–1918

RUDOLF I ——— Anna of Hohenberg
1273–91

ALBERT I ——— Elizabeth of Tyrol
1298–1308

Rudolf
King of Bohemia 1306–07

FREDERICK I
1314–22

Albert II of Austria ——— Johanna von Pfirt

Virida Visconti ——— Leopold III

Albert III of Austria ——— Beatrice
1365–95   of Brandenburg

Cimburca of Masovia ——— Ernest

Johanna ——— Albert IV of Austria
of Bavaria   1395–1404

Eleanora of Portugal ——— FREDERICK III
1440–93

Albert V
King of Hungary 1437
King of Bohemia 1438
Emperor as ALBERT II
1438–39

Ferdinand ——— Isabella   MAXIMILIAN I ——— Mary
King of Spain   Queen of Spain   1493–1519   of Burgundy

Juana of Spain ——————————— Philip the Handsome

Isabella of Portugal ——— CHARLES V   FERDINAND I ——— Anna of Bohemia and Hungary
1519–58   1558–64

Philip II of Spain   Maria ——— MAXIMILIAN II   Mary ——— Charles of Styria
1564–76

Spanish Habsburgs   Anna   RUDOLF II   MATTHIAS   FERDINAND II ——— Maria Anna of Bavaria
1576–1612   1612–19   1619–37

Maria Anna   Mary ——— FERDINAND III
1637–57

Ferdinand Maria   Eleanora ——— LEOPOLD I
of Neuburg   1658–1705

Cunigunde Sobieska ——— Max Emmanuel   JOSEPH I   CHARLES VI ——— Elisabeth Christine of
1705–11   1711–40   Brunswick-Wolfenbüttel

CHARLES VII
1742–45   FRANCIS I ——— MARIA THERESA
1745–65   1740–80

JOSEPH II   Louis XVI ——— Marie Antoinette   LEOPOLD II ——— Maria Luisa
1780–90   of France   1790–92   of Spain

Maria Teresa ——— FRANCIS II
of Naples   1792–1835

Sophia of Bavaria ——— Francis Charles   Napoleon I ——— Marie Louise   FERDINAND I
1835–48

Maximilian   FRANCIS JOSEPH I ——— Elizabeth   Charles Louis ——— Annunziata of Naples
Emperor of Mexico   1848–1916   of Bavaria

Sophie Chotek ——— Francis Ferdinand   Otto ——— Maria Josepha of Saxony
assassinated 1914

CHARLES I
1916–18

MAXIMILIANVS. I. IMP.
ARCHIDVX AVSTRIÆ.
DVX BVRGVNDIÆ

PHILIPPVS. HISP. REX. I.
ARCHIDVX AVSTRIÆ.

MARIA. DVCISSA
BVRGVNDIÆ. MAX: VXOR.

FERDINANDVS. I. IMP.
ARCHIDVX AVSTRIÆ.

CAROLVS. V. IMP.
ARCHIDVX AVSTRIÆ.

LVDOVICVS REX MASS

Ironically, Maximilian I died just one year before his dreams of empire could reach fruition in the person of his grandson Charles. Already king of Spain, Sicily and Naples, Charles was elected Holy Roman emperor in 1520 —becoming, in a stroke, the most powerful ruler in the Western world. This group portrait shows Maximilian with his first wife, Mary of Burgundy; his son Philip; and (left to right) his grandsons Ferdinand, Charles, and Ludwig— all, save Mary, cursed with the protuberant "Habsburg lip." In the simplified genealogy opposite, reign dates are supplied for Holy Roman emperors from 1273 to 1806—and for Austrian monarchs thereafter.

ing Turkish empire grew to encompass land stretching from the Nile to the lower Danube, where it inevitably came into conflict with the Habsburgs. By 1521, a Turkish army of 100,000 men under Sultan Suleiman the Magnificent had conquered Belgrade, crossed the Danube, and was moving toward Hungary. In the royal castle of Buda, high above the Danube, King Louis II and Queen Mary, who had been married only six years before, were blissfully ignorant of the Turkish threat. But Suleiman's advance had not escaped the attention of the royal couple's advisers, who remembered only too well what had happened the year before the children's marriage, when a crusade against the Turks had caused civil war in Hungary. On that occasion a soldier of fortune named George Dózsa had assembled an army of 60,000 men—ostensibly to turn back the Turks—who had instead ravaged the countryside and threatened Buda. Ultimately the peasant rising had been crushed and Dózsa brutally executed, chained to a red-hot iron chair and crowned with a red-hot iron "crown," but the internal damage wrought by the Turks' external threat had not been forgotten.

By the summer of 1526 the Turkish invaders had reached the swampy meadows around Mohács—as always, using the Danube as an invasion route—where young King Louis hoped their advance would be impeded by the swamps and the river. Instead the battle of Mohács, joined on August

51

No sooner had Charles V been elected emperor in the West than a new threat to the Habsburg empire presented itself in the East: a 100,000-man Turkish army under the command of Sultan Suleiman the Magnificent (above) took Belgrade, crossed the Danube, and pressed north toward Budapest.

29, was to become the most disastrous event in Hungary's tortured history. In less than two hours it was all over. Virtually the entire Hungarian army had perished, many in the river and in the swamps, and the casualty list included twenty-year-old Louis. His young queen received the grim news in Vienna, to which she and thousands of Hungarian burghers had fled in horse-drawn carts or in boats. On September 11, Sultan Suleiman and his brother-in-law Ibrahim, the grand vizier, set fire to the twin cities of Buda and Pest and went back home.

After the death of Louis, his brother-in-law Ferdinand fell heir to the thrones of Hungary and Bohemia. Earlier in 1526, Ferdinand had left Spain to take possession of his Austrian dominions, establishing two main branches of the family, one in Austria and the other in Spain. The burghers and the lower nobility of Vienna, most of them Protestants, soon launched an open rebellion against Ferdinand and his Jesuit advisers. From his temporary residence in Wiener Neustadt, Ferdinand dispatched troops to quell the revolt in Vienna, named himself presiding judge of the subsequent tribunal, and ordered the execution of the leaders of the revolt. Vienna's autonomy was rescinded, and the elected city fathers were replaced by appointed civil servants.

In Prague Ferdinand was crowned king of Bohemia, but in Hungary he was opposed by John Zápolya, who had been Louis's regent and was supported by the enemies of the Habsburgs—the Ottoman Empire, France, England, and Venice. Surprisingly, even the pope supported Zápolya. But a few months later Ferdinand marched into Hungary and Zápolya retreated. In November, 1527, Ferdinand was crowned in Buda, despite the fact that he controlled only the western part of the country while Zápolya, with the help of the Turks, ruled over the eastern part.

The rivalry of the two Christians naturally encouraged the Turks to march against Vienna; its fall would open the road toward Western Europe. Accordingly, in May, 1529, a Turkish army of 270,000 men advanced along the north bank of the Danube while Zápolya and his men were ordered to move along the south bank. When the Turks arrived on the outskirts of Vienna on September 21, 1529, they faced a pathetically small defense force of 18,000 men under Count Niklas Salm. The ensuing Turkish siege lasted three weeks, and although the Turks kept the walls and bastions under constant fire, the defenders stood firm. Then, on October 15 the Turks retreated and their Danube flotilla sailed back east. Vienna was saved for the nonce, her peril postponed.

Remaining in the Balkans, the Turks made almost two hundred minor raids into Austrian territory during the next decade, retreating after each foray. Their next chance to mount a major military campaign came after the death of their puppet king, Zápolya, in 1540. They advanced into Buda and on August 26, 1541—the anniversary of the battle of Marchfeld that had established the Habsburgs in Europe almost three hundred years earlier—the Turkish Danube flotilla attacked King Ferdinand's forces entrenched across the river in Pest. The Habsburg troops were badly defeated, and the Turks began an occupation of Hungary's capital that was to last 145 years. Indeed, the country became a province of the Turkish empire, a distant outpost, cut off from the Western thought and culture of its Austrian neighbors. Some modern Hungarian historians believe that their country never quite recovered from the effects of the long occupation.

Ferdinand retained the western areas of the country and his title, king of Hungary, but he failed to recover Buda and the eastern regions. Rather than return to his partitioned capital, Ferdinand remained in Vienna, where he concentrated on the fight against a rapidly spreading Protestantism with the aid of the recently founded Society of Jesus. The Jesuits were masters of psychological persuasion who understood that to win over the Viennese they had to give them entertainment along with religion. The methods of the Spanish Inquisition would not work in Vienna; the shortcut to the hearts of the Viennese was the stage, not the stake, and the Jesuits excelled at theater performances.

The battle against Protestanism in the Hapsburg lands lasted a long time. There were occasional executions, and from time to time booksellers were imprisoned for selling heretical literature, but the Protestants never surrendered; indeed, bold Protestant noblemen are said to have ridden their horses through Saint Stephen's during services. A number of arch-dukes and noblemen—and Ferdinand's son, later Maximilian II—were believed to have been secret Lutherans. In 1618 the long submerged reli-

Suleiman's progress was as methodical as it was menacing, and by 1526 it had become clear to the Hungarians that the Turks' advance had to be checked short of their capital. The test, which came in midsummer at Mohács (below), proved a grotesque mismatch: those Hungarians not drowned in the Danube were slaughtered on its banks. The road to Vienna was now open, and within three years Suleiman's army was threatening the Habsburg capital itself.

gious and political tensions between these two factions surfaced when the Habsburgs' Catholic governors Martinitz and Slawata were thrown from the window of Prague's Hradčany Palace by an irate delegation of the Protestant Czech noblemen. The so-called Defenestration of Prague ended on a note of low comedy—the governors were not seriously hurt because they fell fifty feet into a moat filled with sewage—but the incident suggested the irreconcilable differences that would soon involve all of Europe in war.

The Thirty Years' War, which began in 1618, was dominated by the genius of the Czech Catholic nobleman and mystic Albrecht von Wallenstein who became commander of the imperial army in 1624. Friedrich von Schiller, in his great *Wallenstein* trilogy of 1799, wrote that "his character fluctuates in history." He was called a martyr by some and a demon by others because his huge army lived off the land by robbery and pillage. Ambitious and enigmatic, Wallenstein listened only to his astrologers, especially Johannes Kepler of Regensburg. At the height of his power in the early 1630s, Wallenstein had scored a number of decisive military victories over the Protestants and was actually Prague's "secret king." He received messages and tempting offers from all the courts in Europe—the French once promised him a million livres a year if he would turn against the Habsburg emperor—and he built himself one of the city's most beautiful baroque palaces. There he stayed for weeks at a time, locked in his dark study, trying to divine the future from the predictions of his astrologers.

Mysticism has always been a strong force in Prague, hovering over its dim churches and about such statues as that of John of Nepomuk, patron saint of Bohemia, and such gravestones as that of Jehuda Liva ben Bezalel, the Rabbi Löw who died in 1609 and is buried in Prague's Old Jewish Cemetery. According to legend, it was Löw, a student of the cabala, who created the golem, a clay robot that did hard work, carried water, and cleaned the streets. Wallenstein certainly belonged in such a mystical city. Ultimately he did betray his emperor—briefly—before turning on the emperor's enemies and driving them out of Prague. As Swedish King Gustavus Adolfus and his vanquished Protestant army retreated, Wallenstein secretly contacted the Swedes, indicating that he was ready to betray the emperor once again. This time, however, Ferdinand II moved faster than his faithless general, having Wallenstein assassinated in Bohemia in 1634.

Year after year the terrible war dragged on, with many battles fought along the Bavarian Danube. Fronts shifted, with victories and defeats radically altering the map of Europe. Provinces changed hands, but no one profited because the villages and towns involved had been reduced to heaps of rubble. In 1648, thirty years after the Defenestration of Prague, the senseless war ended with the Treaty of Westphalia, which humiliated the Habsburgs and insured further conflicts in their polyglot empire. At least ten million people had died, and the devastation throughout much of Central Europe was complete.

In Vienna the citizenry expressed its relief that the war had finally ended through stone—in exultant statues and palaces. Some pessimists worried about the vague possibility of another Turkish invasion, but most people

enjoyed the superpageants in which practically the entire populace took part. There were, among other things, writes Robert Haas, "Jesuit dramas, banquets and balls, Italian and Spanish comedies, a ballet performed by the nobility introducing twelve Ethiopian beauties whose jewellery was of untold value," and "two full-length equestrian ballets. . . ."

Ferdinand III, who died in 1657, is remembered in music-minded Austria not for signing the Treaty of Westphalia but as the first patron of opera. His third wife, Eleonora Gonzaga, had inherited a passion for opera from her father, the duke of Mantua. (Claudio Monteverdi, the first operatic genius, had performed his early masterpieces in Mantua.) And she, in turn, passed that passion on to her offspring. Thus when Ferdinand's successor, Leopold I, married his first wife, Margaret Theresa of Spain, the nuptial production of *Il Pomo d'Oro* ("The Golden Apple") by Marc' Antonio Cesti ran for an entire year. Two Italian architects built the new Theater auf der Cortina for the show, which cost 300,000 guilders and had sixty-seven scenes, fifty soloists, and a cast of one thousand.

Leopold I, a noted composer himself, is now fondly remembered as "the most musical Habsburg." (According to a Viennese legend, he felt his death approaching and ordered the *Hofmusikkapelle* to perform his favorite compositions in an adjoining hall, dying peacefully while the music welled around him.) Leopold was an absolute monarch of the Baroque Age, and he justly considered music and opera to be expressions of imperial power. His marriage was a typical Habsburg affair. Margaret, the second daughter of King Philip IV of Spain, was first in line to succeed her father —an artfully contrived diplomatic arrangement designed to thwart the imperial ambitions of Louis XIV of France, who had married Philip's first-born daughter, Marie Thérèse. When this arrangement broke down, as it was bound to do, the War of the Spanish Succession became inevitable.

As political fortunes shifted during the Thirty Years' War, so did the mercurial loyalties of Albrecht von Wallenstein (above, left), an ambitious, enigmatic Czech nobleman who twice betrayed his emperor before the latter had him assassinated in 1634. By that time formal displays of equine pageantry, such as the one seen opposite, had given way to grim scenes of pillage and bombardment (above). In the space of three decades, ten million lives had been lost and virtually every village in the Danube Basin had been destroyed.

With characteristic joie de vivre *the irrepressibly optimistic Viennese celebrated the conclusion of the Thirty Years' War in stone and song, building new theaters to showcase the city's newest cultural diversion, opera. This civic idyll was to prove tragically brief, however: three decades after the war's end, catastrophe of another sort was visited upon the city. By the time the cholera epidemic of 1679 had run its course, 70,000 Viennese had died and Emperor Leopold I had pledged to erect a monument commemorating his capital's deliverance from the plague. As good as his word, this most musical of all Habsburg monarchs commissioned the Pestsäule (right), a baroque column embellished with gruesome scenes from the plague year (detail above).*

This conflict led not only to permanent antagonism between Austria and France but, most ominously, to a rapprochement between France and Turkey. From nearby Hungary the Turks were making sporadic raids into Austria, and at one point Leopold had to go to Regensburg to ask the German Diet for soldiers, arms, and financial support against his enemies —a distasteful task for a man who would rather have composed music.

In 1679 Vienna suffered the worst cholera epidemic in its history. According to Abraham a Sancta Clara, the Augustinian court friar from Swabia who combined jokes with religion and fun with preaching, more than 70,000 people died of the plague. The emperor, his court, and the rich left town; the poor stayed and many died. Pompous state processions were met at intersections "by carriages with piles of dead bodies . . . a truly apocalyptic contrast." Among the bodies were people who were merely sick or dead-drunk. A much-loved legend tells of the popular singer, Augustin Marx, who cherished the improbable but pleasurable theory that wine protected one against the plague. Marx simply got drunk and stayed drunk. After passing out one day, he was carted off with the dead and thrown into the plague pit. Chronicler P. Fuhrmann reports that Augustin "woke up in the morning . . . stepping on the dead, and finally was rescued by the *Ziehknechte*, who after dawn appeared with other dead bodies and helped him out. . . ." He is remembered in the popular folksong, "Ach, du lieber Augustin, alles ist hin" (Oh, my dear Augustin, everything's gone), that remains the leitmotiv of Vienna's cheerful pessimism.

Paul de Sorbait, rector of Vienna University, wrote about the sanitary conditions in town, "where dead dogs, cats and fowl were thrown into the street. . . goats were kept in living rooms because their smell is said to suck up the germs of the plague." Dr. Sorbait suggested his own anticholera therapy, the ringing of church bells—"because this will clean the air and move the winds that have been locked in. . . . Yes, the bells will drive out the evil spirits that float through the air." But Sorbait had little confidence in his own prescription, and when things got really bad he and most other local doctors fled the city. Criminals had to be released from jail to bury the dead, and not until winter came did the epidemic subside.

By August, 1682, Vienna was in danger of being engulfed by another form of plague. Sultan Mohammed IV, after consulting with his grand vizier, Kara Mustafa, had decided to disregard the peace treaty with Austria signed in 1664 and launch a campaign before the treaty expired in 1684. The Turks gambled that the dissension among the German princes, the jealousies among Austria's allies, and the hostility between Leopold I and Louis XIV had so weakened the Habsburgs that they could not mount an effective defense. And thus, in July, 1683, a Turkish army of about 275,000 men, with some irregular Magyar and Tartar forces, arrived outside Vienna, throwing the city into a panic. Emperor Leopold, his grandees and court officials, and some 60,000 Viennese fled in undignified haste. Leopold went first to Krems and later moved farther up the Danube to Linz. The imperial forces under the duke of Lorraine, a scholarly strategist, were considered too weak to stop the Turks, which meant that until Leopold's allies, particularly King John III Sobieski of Poland, could send their troops, Vienna would have to depend on its own garrison. As during the siege of 1529, the scorched-earth policy once more went into force and Vienna's suburbs were razed to shorten the city's line of defense.

On July 14, the Turks surrounded the city, and Kara Mustafa asked the defenders to surrender. "Deliver the fortress and live in peace under the Sultan as Christians," he commanded; ". . . if you resist, death and spoliation and slavery shall be the fate of all!" Count Ernst Rüdiger von Starhemberg, who became the hero of the siege, provided Vienna's answer: he ordered the city gates walled up. Starhemberg's garrison consisted of 16,000 men—regular soldiers and a militia made up of students, merchants, burghers, and a few court officials who had decided to stay. He also had three hundred guns inside the walls. The Turkish forward units were encamped a mere 450 paces away, and the much-feared Janissaries, who never took prisoners and systematically massacred their enemies, were just outside the walls, facing the Burg and Löwel bastions.

There had been much loose talk of a glorious victory in Kara Mustafa's headquarters tent, but it took the Turks three weeks just to reach the edge of the counterscarp, which was reinforced with iron spikes. The fight for the walled city began on August 6, but there was no panic inside this time. The defenders had simply made up their minds: they would rather die than live under the Turkish crescent. There was still enough food and when incendiary bombs fell, the fire brigade went quickly into action. Schools were closed but churches stayed open. Morale was high.

When the Turks cut the fresh-water conduits into the city, an epidemic of dysentery ensued, however, and it soon became difficult to get rid of the garbage that was piling up inside the walls. Outside the city, the Magyars and Tartars were looting and killing in a calculated effort to break down the spirit of the defenders. Despite these obstacles, Count Starhemberg managed to establish contact with the outside world through messengers, one of whom, a skilled Polish double agent named Franz Kolschitzky, disguised himself as a Turk, reached the headquarters of the duke of Lorraine in Lower Austria, and reported on the situation inside Vienna. After the siege, Kolschitzky published a rather sensational account of his adventures that created "enthusiasm mingled with skepticism."

On September 4 a Turkish mine tore a large hole in the wall of the Burg bastion. Turkish troops and Janissaries shouted "Allah!" and stormed through the gap, and for some eighty minutes the fate of Vienna hung in a precarious balance. Starhemberg ordered his elite troops to counterattack, and the Turks were eventually beaten back. The specter of defeat had been temporarily banished, but the general situation was desperate indeed. There was little water and less food left, and the beleaguered townspeople had been reduced to eating their donkeys and cats. Day and night, observers on top of the tower of Saint Stephen's watched the hills of the Wienerwald, praying that the relieving armies would come before it was too late.

At dawn on September 11 the sentries' long vigil was rewarded: allied troops appeared atop the Leopoldsberg and Kahlenberg, prominent hills in the Wienerwald. Flares went up, signaling to the exhausted defenders inside the walls that relief was near. Too late Kara Mustafa realized his terrible mistake: intent on capturing Vienna, he had deployed his elite troops near the city walls and had neglected to keep the hills around Vienna under control. Suddenly he was caught between the imperial forces on the hills and the defenders inside the city walls, who now prepared their long-awaited counteroffensive against the Turks.

The final battle began at dawn on September 12 with a series of confusing and inconclusive encounters. "We fought from ridge to valley and from valley to ridge," a general later said. The duke of Lorraine ordered an attack against the right wing of the Turks; Ibrahim Pasha, the sultan's brother-in-law, ordered his men to withdraw and regroup for a counterattack. His decision was the right one, but the Turkish counterattack never came. Around noon the duke of Lorraine held a short strategy session with his commanders. King John III Sobieski of Poland, a powerful ally, suggested a pause in the fighting. The supreme commander and most generals wanted to exploit their tactical advantage before the Turks could regroup, and the duke of Lorraine agreed to continue the battle. By this time his advance units were only two miles from the city walls.

The decisive attack began at 3:20 P.M., "in the fierce heat of the afternoon," with the imperial troops and Saxons storming forward. Soon thereafter King John's Polish cavalry broke through the Turkish lines and reached the encampment of the grand vizier. In a masterful move, the duke of Lorraine then swung wide to the right, pushing the Turks toward the center of the front just as the Saxons arrived on the left. Kara Mustafa, sensing that all was lost, opted for a desperate retreat toward Hungary, throwing roughly 20,000 of his best cavalrymen against the Poles. But it was too little and too late, and by 4:00 P.M. the Turks were in wild flight along the entire front. Inside the walled city, Starhemberg ordered the gates opened and gave his men orders to attack the hated Janissaries.

It was 5:30 P.M. when trumpets at the Schottentor announced the arrival of the first units of the imperial army, two dragoon regiments under the margrave of Baden. After seventy-two days, Vienna was free again; the city, and with it Western Europe, had once again been saved from the Turks. Emperor Leopold I, who had by this time retreated as far as Passau, now returned to Vienna, where he was welcomed by all commanders except the arrogant Polish king. When he reached his palace, the Hofburg, and saw the devastation, he wept—and a few days later he issued a series of decrees that contained more reprimand than praise. He specifically forbade "hatred, envy, fancy dresses, gossip. . . and immorality, all of which have been widely practised." Count Starhemberg he called "the saviour of the Holy Roman Empire and of Europe," which was certainly true. A petition of the burghers asking for the guns the Turks had left behind was turned down by the imperial bureaucrats (who had fled Vienna during the siege). Later the Turkish cannons were cast into a large bell, the *Pummerin*, which was hoisted up to the spire of Saint Stephen's, a constant reminder of the great city's near-disaster.

OVERLEAF: *In 1683, another kind of plague threatened to engulf Vienna: a Turkish army of some 275,000 men laid seige to the city. By early September Kara Mustafa's troops had breached the city's walls and were gathering for a final assault. But before the Turks could strike, an allied expeditionary force arrived on the scene. A contemporary view of the rout that followed shows French and Polish troops (left) putting Kara Mustafa's feared Janissaries to flight. Picking his way across the battlefield some hours later, a sharp-eyed Pole named Kolschitzky stumbled upon two bags of unroasted Turkish coffee beans. With those beans as his sole inventory, Kolschitzky opened the first of Vienna's many coffeehouses.*

4

Rise of the Habsburgs

*T*he allied army that lifted the second Turkish siege of Vienna and routed the troops of Kara Mustafa included among its officers a twenty-year-old French prince described by a contemporary as "small and ugly." His name was François-Eugène de Savoie-Carignan, but he is remembered simply as Prince Eugene, Austria's secret emperor, great soldier, and folk hero. Although he never bothered to learn German and signed his name trilingually, Eugenio von Savoye, he was the last great builder of the Habsburg Danube monarchy.

It is useless to speculate on what might have happened if Louis XIV had granted the young man's application for a colonel's commission in the French army. Turned down, Prince Eugene came to Vienna and offered his services to Emperor Leopold I, who wisely accepted. In the years that followed, Eugene issued repeated warnings to the emperor—and later to Leopold's successors, Joseph I and Charles VI—that the Turks would attempt a comeback unless they were decisively defeated along the lower Danube, where they had built a base of power that reached as far west as Belgrade. In 1697 and again in 1716 Eugene was permitted to lead small expeditionary forces against the Turks, but not until 1717, under Charles VI, was he given a free rein to strike deep into Turkish-held territory. That time he led an army of 100,000 men and a flotilla of fifty craft down the Danube. Near Pančevo the army crossed the river, and the prince deployed his forces east of Belgrade, where his engineers began erecting the Eugene Line, a semicircle of ramparts and trenches from the banks of the Sava to the banks of the Danube. He also built pontoon bridges across both rivers and trained his artillery on Belgrade with its 30,000 defenders. Meanwhile, however, a Turkish army of 200,000 was forming an encircling crescent just beyond the outer perimeter of the Eugene Line. With his forces outnumbered two to one, the Habsburg commander's position was indeed precarious. Prince Eugene nonetheless ordered an attack early on the morning of August 16. Since it was still dark and a heavy fog was rising from the two rivers, there was widespread confusion. At one point the Turks broke through the imperial forces and seemed likely to divide and conquer the

Austrians. Risking all, Eugene threw his reserves into the center—and routed the Turkish forces. By eleven o'clock it was all over, and the next day Belgrade surrendered. A famous Austrian folk song, "Prinz Eugen, der edle Ritter," tells of "the noble knight" who built a bridge across the Danube and recovered the fortress of Belgrade for the empire. The subsequent peace treaty established the Habsburgs in the Balkans for almost two hundred years, but it also created the multinational problems that led to the breakup of the empire at the end of World War I.

In Vienna Prince Eugene is also remembered as the city's greatest patron of the arts during the post-siege era. He did for baroque Vienna what the Medicis accomplished for Florence during the Renaissance. Vienna, he insisted, must become the eastern citadel of Christian civilization, and to achieve this she must be militarily secure. To this end he ordered the construction of the Line Wall, which enclosed both the walled inner city and the suburbs. Essentially, Vienna remains today as it looked to Prince Eugene: the old city is the bull's eye of a vast dartboard, with several circles—the Ringstrasse, the inner and outer Gürtel—around it. Saint Stephen's stands at the very heart of the city. Unlike most German cities, which are built outward from large central squares, Vienna is round in shape and ringed by circular avenues.

With the completion of the Line Wall, Eugene turned toward more pleasant projects. He began by commissioning two great builders, Johann Bernard Fischer von Erlach and Johann Lucas von Hildebrandt, to put up a winter palace for him in Himmelpfortgasse near Saint Stephen's, an easy walk from the Hofburg, the imperial palace. The two artists created a masterpiece of restrained grandeur on the narrow site Eugene had chosen. The portals were flanked by shallow bas-reliefs which clearly showed that the prince knew his worth: the reliefs were scenes from the myth of Hercules. Restraint was nowhere in evidence inside the palace, with its magnificent staircase, stone giants supporting the landings, and beautiful state rooms.

A biased but amusing observer of Vienna in this period, Lady Mary Wortley Montagu, wife of the British ambassador to Turkey, writes in her *Embassy Letters* that "the streets [are] very close, and so narrow, one cannot observe the fine fronts of the palaces, though many of them very well deserve observation, being truly magnificent. . . ." But when one entered, there was luxury, "richly carved and gilt, and the furniture such as is seldom seen in the palaces of sovereign princes in other countries—the hangings are the finest tapestry of Brussels . . . and window curtains of the richest Genoa damask or velvet, almost covered with gold lace. . . ."

Vienna's building boom during the early eighteenth century was not sponsored by the often thrifty Habsburgs but by rich aristocrats, leading Montesquieu to describe Austria as "the land in which the subjects are better housed than their ruler." The Turkish siege had destroyed many fine buildings, but since the Turks were gone forever—or so the popular consensus held—the rich were eager to give concrete form to their country's new prosperity and prominence. Austria's economic structure was notoriously unsound, however, and there was no confidence in the financial strength of

Charles VI, last male member of the House of Habsburg, devoted the bulk of his reign to a series of ultimately futile attempts to dictate the Polish and Spanish successions. He fared better in his efforts to ensure that his daughter Maria Theresa would inherit his crown. An ivory statuette carved in 1711, the year of Charles's accession, shows the young emperor, mounted on a Lipizzaner stallion, saluting a kneeling representation of the state of Austria.

the Habsburgs, who were often in debt to moneylenders. Sooner or later, pessimists said, the Danube empire would collapse financially, which made it fruitless to save one's money. It made much better sense to invest in real estate, buy beautiful sites, and put up palaces—and thus baroque Vienna was created. Some of the great palaces survive as schools or institutes, among them Prince Eugene's winter palace which has housed the Ministry of Finance for some 150 years. Only a few families—the Harrachs, the Liechtensteins—still own their palaces and art treasures.

Many eighteenth-century noblemen became dilettantish architects, building their own monuments. Count Friedrich Carl Schönborn admitted that the building craze was "a devilish passion, but once you have started, you cannot stop. What," he asked, "would happen to artists and artisans whom God created if He did not also create fools to support them?" Most of the artisans who created eighteenth-century Vienna were from Italy, and they were fast workers. Marble was rarely used; more often a mixture of plaster, lime, and sand was employed. Such stucco was flexible—it was almost like building for the stage. Indeed, Vienna became an oversized stage where nearly everybody was performing a part. "Baroque" originally meant something that was flamboyant and bizarre—theatrical. It began as an architectural style, but it eventually became a state of mind in Vienna.

"The great baroque architects . . . were like actors—actors with a touch of genius," wrote Karl Scheffler. This was indisputably true of the first architect on Eugene's winter palace, Fischer von Erlach, who was born in Graz, Styria, and worked in Rome for sixteen years as a pupil of Giovanni Lorenzo Bernini. Fischer von Erlach began his career by "Italianizing" suburban houses, but his great ambition was to build a summer palace for the Habsburgs that would be more grandiose than Versailles. The Habsburgs, however, were not as flamboyant as Louis XIV, and Fischer's original blueprint for an imperial summer palace, the Schönbrunn, was severely revised and reduced. It is a great palace, nonetheless, especially when Mozart is performed in its courtyard or chamber music is played in its cavernous Great Gallery.

Fischer von Erlach's masterpiece, Vienna's famous Karlskirche, was built to fulfill a vow made by Emperor Charles VI during the plague of 1713. Erected to honor the emperor's patron saint, Saint Carlo Borromeo, the church was placed on an elevation above Karlsplatz, dominating the square below. The entrance is flanked by two Trajanesque columns with spiral bas-reliefs showing scenes from the life of Saint Carlo. Pomp and flamboyance dominate the interior walls of the church and its immense cupola.

The pious call Karlskirche a "theatrical" church, and it is indisputably ill-suited to quiet prayer. On the other hand, Vienna's greatest church and the city's symbol, Saint Stephen's, is Gothic—solemn and austere. The first parish church of Saint Stephen's, built on a site ceded to the city in 1137 by the bishop of Passau, burned to the ground some years later. In 1290, after the Habsburgs had made Vienna their capital, the building of the great cathedral was begun to demonstrate the city's exalted position in the Christian world. It was started in Romanesque style—the ancient Romanesque front is now the main entrance on Saint Stephen's Square—and was later expanded in Gothic style, which remains dominant although baroque

Johann Bernard Fischer von Erlach began his long career in Rome, where he was apprenticed for sixteen years to Giovanni Bernini, the designer of Saint Peter's and indisputably the century's most influential architect. As a result, the master's style is everywhere evident in the lines of Fischer von Erlach's masterpiece, Vienna's Karlskirche— from its soaring cupola (below) to its dramatic high altar (below, left).

details also show up, always harmoniously, in many spots. The southern tower is a tall, powerful pyramid; the northern tower, never completed, remains truncated, capped by a copper lid. Originally, of course, the cathedral was to have twin towers; but the builders ran out of funds, and by the time they had raised more the Gothic era had ended. The Viennese would consider it as absurd to finish Saint Stephen's second tower now as to finish Schubert's *Unfinished Symphony*.

Few churches in Vienna are lauded by architectural purists because most of them are mixtures of styles. The noble exceptions are Saint Ruprecht's, supposedly the oldest, which is pure late-Romanesque; the Gothic Saint Maria am Gestade, which Napoleon's soldiers were to use as a powder magazine; and the early Gothic Augustinerkirche near the Hofburg, where the hearts of deceased Habsburg rulers were interred.

In 1712, while Prince Eugene was planning his Turkish campaign, one Josef Anton Stranitzky, "licensed tooth breaker and mouth doctor," was

granted the privilege of managing the new Kärntnertor Theater (near today's State Opera), where he presented a succession of immensely popular "Hanswurst" comedies. Hanswurst, the Viennese version of Jack-pudding, was a stock figure—part comic, part parodist and social critic, a mixture always popular in Vienna. So taken was the public with these performances that ladies and gentlemen at court frequently slipped away from a boring evening of Italian opera to be regaled by Hanswurst. Quite naturally, Stranitzky prospered, and after a few years he was able to open several new theaters and abandon dentistry altogether. After Charles VI's death, Hanswurst comedies were forbidden by imperial decree; but soon thereafter a new chapter appeared on the theatrical scene, a shrewd Austrian peasant named Kasperl who was at once a comedian and satirist—in short, Hanswurst incarnate.

No evidence exists that Prince Eugene ever went to see one of the farcical plays; he was probably too busy, both as a soldier and as a builder. He

Bernardo Bellotto's vista of Vienna from the Upper Belvedere (above) is framed by the dome of Karlskirche on the left and that of a nunnery on the right. The middle distance is bisected by the single spire of Saint Stephen's, to the left of which lie the Vienna Woods. No less spectacular are the Belvedere's interiors, which include a formal salon (far left) dominated by a heroic statue of Prince Eugene himself.

67

had commissioned Lucas von Hildebrandt, Fischer von Erlach's foremost rival, to build him a summer palace on the finest site in Vienna, a gently ascending slope overlooking Saint Stephen's, the city, the river, and the Wienerwald that lies beyond. Before construction had even begun, Hildebrandt sent for a French artisan from the Bavarian court and had formal gardens laid out on the slope. At its foot he built the Lower Belvedere, deceivingly simple from the outside, almost a bungalow, but with living quarters extravagantly decorated in gold and marble and silk. Then on top of the slope he built the beautiful and graceful Upper Belvedere.

Prince Eugene filled Hildebrandt's masterpiece with art treasures and rare books, and there he gave great receptions at which he wore his hat as he received foreign dignitaries—an arrogant assumption of the emperor's prerogative. No wonder, then, that Charles VI at last bent an ear to the anti-Eugene faction at his court. And that when the old soldier warned that Prussia might well become the next grave threat to the Habsburgs, Charles refused to listen. The anti-Eugene faction spread the word that the old soldier was losing his senses. Prussia, although it reached from the Baltic to Silesia, had only two million people, little more than a tenth of imperial Austria's population. A threat? Ridiculous!

Perhaps Prince Eugene no longer cared; his place in history was secure. He received as friends the philosophers Leibniz and Voltaire, and Jean Baptiste Rousseau, his court poet. He never married, but in his later years he acquired a dear friend, Countess Lory Batthyány, with whom he spent many quiet evenings playing piquet. According to legend, Prince Eugene, who was by this time more than seventy, often fell asleep while being driven to the small Batthyány Palace, another Fischer masterpiece. Eugene's coachman and lackey, also septuagenarians, would likewise doze off, but the horses knew the route and always stopped in front of the palace. People walked by and smiled; no one would have thought of disturbing the sleep of the three old gentlemen.

Prince Eugene died in 1736. Developments in Prussia already indicated that the old soldier had been right, and that the Habsburgs might have to pay dearly for having failed to heed his advice. In 1713 Frederick William I had become ruler of Prussia, where he soon established himself as *Soldatenkönig*, "the soldiers' king" who made militarism his state religion. He wanted to make Prussia a great military power in Europe, a concept that he pursued with almost religious fervor, believing it to be his sacred duty. His soldiers were drilled to march farther and shoot faster; the officers' corps became a state within the state.

The threat that such overweening militarism posed to the Habsburg empire was palpable, but no one in Vienna cared to notice it. Emperor Charles VI was more worried about the fact that he was without a male heir, and that there was no agreement among the legal experts as to whether his eldest daughter, Maria Theresa, could succeed him. In a bold attempt to resolve this thorny diplomatic question, the emperor's ministers drew up the Pragmatic Sanction, a complex legal document designed to ratify both matrilineal succession and the territorial integrity of the Habs-

The "glorious superfluity" of the baroque era achieved its apotheosis in the Upper Belvedere—which, despite its size, was never intended as a residence. Lucas von Hildebrandt designed this absolutely symmetrical warren of elegant reception rooms for Prince Eugene, who used it exclusively for entertaining.

burg empire. To have any hope of succeeding, the Sanction had to be guaranteed not only by all estates within the Habsburg empire but by all major foreign powers. The emperor's legal advisers assured him that this could be achieved. Only Prince Eugene had dissented: what Maria Theresa would need to confirm her right to the throne, he had said, was a good army and a few victories on the battlefield. As usual, he was right.

By the time Charles VI died in 1740, France had become determined to reduce Austria's power, and Charles Albert, the elector of Bavaria, claimed some right to become Holy Roman emperor as a descendant of the oldest daughter of Ferdinand I. Frederick II of Prussia (now known as Frederick the Great)—who hated "that woman" on the Habsburg throne—promptly defeated Maria Theresa's soldiers and annexed Silesia. Despite such setbacks, Maria Theresa held her own in Vienna, and in 1745 she had her husband, Francis of Lorraine, crowned Emperor Francis I. As a young woman, Maria Theresa had been a celebrated beauty, but giving birth to sixteen children, ten of whom survived infancy, left her an overweight matron. She ran her empire as a thrifty housewife runs her home, and although she longed to get Silesia back, she could not bring herself to finance the necessary military forces.

Emperor Joseph II, Maria Theresa's oldest son and successor, is thought of as a great reformer, a monarch of enlightened absolutism, although in his later years he was forced by the Church and the narrow-minded court aristocracy to revise or partially rescind many of his early reforms. He began his short reign (1780–90) by proclaiming an edict of tolerance that granted Protestants the right to practice their religion privately, to become burghers, and to hold academic degrees. Jews were permitted to become craftsmen and farmers; their children were admitted to Christian schools and priests were admonished to preach the equality of Jews.

Concurrently, in an attempt to exercise greater control over the Church, Joseph abolished seven religious orders, closed 738 monasteries and convents, and expelled foreign monks and nuns. Rome became alarmed and Pope Pius VI came to Vienna in person to try to dissuade the emperor from his radical reforms. This he failed to do, although large crowds gathered wherever he appeared. Yet things had changed: when the pope blessed a crowd from the balcony of a Jesuit church, Josef Blumauer, an irreverent local poet and playwright, kept his hat on. The emperor further infuriated the Vatican when he claimed the right to nominate bishops and archbishops—and he did so in Milan, despite the pope's protest. He also suppressed ecclesiastical establishments and established secular schools.

Joseph II's social reforms were even more far-reaching. The tax system was revised. Joseph Sonnenfels, who as minister of justice under Maria Theresa had seen to it that torture was abolished, now pleaded with Joseph for the abolition of censorship and capital punishment. The emperor agreed to change the civil and penal codes, and henceforth the death penalty was limited to murder and rebellion.

Sonnenfels is perhaps best remembered today for his saying: "Spectacles are necessary." This was something Joseph II understood very well,

Although her accession to the Austrian throne in 1740 was greeted with widespread derision, Maria Theresa proved to be a capable if cautious monarch, one whose forty-year reign was marked by stability and prosperity. The group portrait opposite, painted in 1750, shows the empress with eleven of the sixteen children she bore her husband and co-regent, Francis of Lorraine. Repeated confinements eventually robbed Maria Theresa of her looks, but not of her taste for elaborate dresses and intricate bijoux such as the bouquet ·of precious stones seen at far left. To celebrate the recapture of Prague in 1743, the empress staged a spectacular "carousel" in the great hall of Vienna's renowned Spanish Riding School (opposite, below), home of the Lipizzaners. Clad in a golden riding habit, Maria Theresa herself led the first quadrille.

It took Napoleon's brilliant engineer, Count Bertrand, just a fortnight to throw a small pontoon bridge across the Danube—and it took the seasoned French army even less time to cross the river (above) and seize the inadequately defended Austrian capital in 1809.

Parma, Piacenza, and Custoza. After her death she was buried in Vienna next to her ill-fated son.

After Napoleon was exiled to Elba, the brilliant Austrian statesman and diplomat Prince Metternich was to host the victorious allies at the Congress of Vienna. Talleyrand came from Paris, bringing along his great chef, Carême, after informing Louis XVIII that he had "more need of casseroles than of written instructions." England was represented by Lord Castlereagh and the Duke of Wellington. In addition, innumerable minor kings and princes, many ambassadors, and perhaps 100,000 visitors gathered in Vienna. The allies, who stuck together through years of travail, immediately set to bickering. Nonetheless, the Congress of Vienna created a new order for Europe, one that lasted almost a hundred years—though the gathering is still best remembered for the *bon mot* of Prince Charles Joseph von Ligne, a highly unsuccessful general under the Habsburgs, "Le congrès danse, mais il ne marche pas" (the congress dances but does not march). The popular dance was, of course, the waltz, a genuine Viennese creation, and for a few months, at least, Vienna was truly the capital of Europe.

The years between the Congress of Vienna, which was convened in 1814, and the great revolutions of 1848 are now known as Vienna's Biedermeier era. The word was derived from the satirical poems published in the journal *Fliegende Blätter*, attributed to a fictitious Swabian schoolteacher, Gottlieb Biedermayer, who pretended to cherish the *Gemütlichkeit* of quiet bourgeois life. Many now think of the era as Vienna's golden age, although for the bulk of the city's residents it was neither golden nor *gemütlich*. Emperor Francis II and Prince Metternich, who jointly oversaw Austria's destiny, have often been portrayed as benevolent, but both had been deeply perturbed by the French Revolution and had determined that such a catastrophe must never be permitted to occur in the Habsburg empire. Metternich envisioned the restoration of the old order; he had the flexibility of the true statesman in external affairs, but inside Austria he demanded rigid adherence to established norms. His most powerful intimate was Friedrich von Gentz of Silesia, who once wrote to Metternich he was proud that neither freedom of opinion nor the "hideous spectre of the freedom of the press" were allowed in Vienna.

In 1831 a book of poems, *Rambles of a Viennese Poet*, was anonymously published in Hamburg and immediately banned in Vienna. The poet had elegantly attacked the reactionary police system of Metternich. The author, Count Anton Alexander von Auersperg, was widely known and was one of several poets and playwrights who rebelled against the *Gemütlichkeit* of Biedermeier Vienna. Among them were Ferdinand Raimund, a playwright and actor, and Emanuel Schikaneder, a highly popular comedian before he became the librettist of Mozart's *Die Zauberflöte*. The Viennese recognized themselves in Raimund's melancholic characters and appreciated his plays with their mixture of comedy and resignation, their cheerfulness even in moments of despair. Raimund's most famous play was *Der Verschwender* ("The Spendthrift"), which he called, somewhat deceivingly, a magic tale; actually it is the tragedy of a young spendthrift who ruins his family and himself and winds up as a beggar.

Raimund's unhappiness at becoming a comic rather than a tragic author

By 1814, the Corsican conqueror's empire was in tatters, he himself was imprisoned on Elba, and Europe's preeminent statesman, Prince Metternich, was hosting the Congress of Vienna. A contemporary view of that gathering shows Metternich, who was then at the apogee of his powers, introducing the Duke of Wellington (seated, far left) to Talleyrand (second from the right).

was not alleviated by the success of his competitor, Johann Nestroy, who abandoned a career in opera to become Austria's greatest satirical playwright. He too acted in his own plays, and as a result the Viennese, who thrive on artistic rivalry, soon divided into Raimund fans and Nestroy fans. In his early plays Nestroy attacked the phony coziness of what was often called "the fried chicken era," which referred to a delicacy particularly popular at the time. Nestroy knew how to make people laugh about serious things—the secret of all Viennese moralists since Abraham a Sancta Clara—but it nonetheless took courage for him to write *Freiheit im Krähwinkel,* a bitter satire on the 1848 revolution.

The poets of the Biedermeier were lonely men. Raimund and Adalbert Stifter committed suicide, and Nestroy suffered from long attacks of melancholy. Nikolaus Lenau, a great lyrical poet, suffered fits of depression that ended in madness. And Franz Grillparzer, one of the great German-language dramatists, eventually retired into gloomy seclusion. Grillparzer, who saw clearly that Metternich's rule would lead to chaos, rebelled when Metternich announced that he wanted to create a French-style national academy. "It is—may God forgive me—as though the devil were to build a church," Grillparzer said. Shortly thereafter, a committee of writers and intellectuals that included Grillparzer presented Metternich with a petition against censorship; their real desire, of course, was to get rid of Metternich. With his customary arrogance, the prince declared that he didn't know what a committee meant.

Of the 1848 revolutions that changed life all over Europe, Vienna's was the longest, seven-and-a-half months, and the most frustrating. It began on March 13 but was preceded by the *Vormärz,* the pre-March period when sensitive people felt that something was about to happen. The portents were readily visible during this early stage, especially in the Polish, Hungarian, and Italian provinces of the Habsburg empire, where the forces of nationalism were getting stronger. Poland had been partitioned numerous times, with czarist Russia and Austria receiving the largest shares. An uprising of Polish patriots against Russia in 1831 had been drowned in blood, but much unrest remained in Galicia, the Austrian part of Poland, and consequently Metternich had sent troops there. In 1846 the free city of Kraków was placed under strict military rule by the Austrian commander. There was also danger in Hungary, where Ferencz Deák was calling for an independent Hungarian government and Lajos Kossuth had come close to rebellion by demanding the establishment of a Hungarian republic. Nationalism was spreading in northern Italy as well, and the Austrians were obliged to keep a large force stationed there; non-Italian soldiers were selected for this job so that they could not be talked into mutiny by the Italian patriots. In the cities, Austrian officers were privately hated and publicly ignored. In Venice's Piazza San Marco they walked on one side of the great plaza, the Italians on the other.

All this was, of course, reported to Metternich, who somehow failed to read the signs correctly. Life in Vienna seemed deceptively quiet during the months preceding the revolution. Chroniclers noted that the carnival

When he entered Vienna at the head of his conquering army, Napoleon took up residence in the old Hofburg Palace at the city's center. A day later he moved to Schönbrunn, which he clearly found more to his liking. Commissioned by Leopold I and designed by the redoubtable Fischer von Erlach, this sprawling royal residence on the city's western perimeter was sumptuous even by the French emperor's standards. The inlaid and overpainted walls of the salon at left, for example, are reported to have cost a million taler.

OVERLEAF: Despite the fact that it contains more than 1,400 rooms, Schönbrunn is a remarkably unimposing edifice. Its splendid gardens and familiar "Schönbrunn yellow" façade seem to reflect Vienna's special Gemütlichkeit.

season that year was particularly brilliant, and late in 1847 the historian, painter, and illustrator Wilhelm von Kaulbach wrote to his wife, "Vienna is a city of sensuous pleasures and Strauss the sun around which everything turns." Actually there were two waltz kings named Strauss: the older, now called Johann Strauss the Elder, and his son, the great Johann Strauss. The air seemed filled with Strauss melodies. Indeed, there was so much music in Vienna that people found little time to talk about the poorer suburbs, where bakeries were plundered and soup kitchens for the very poor had been set up in 1847. A working man's day was fourteen hours and did not earn him a living wage—this at a time when Vienna's intoxicated rich were cheering young Strauss's "Bacchus Polka." People who claimed to have no money to pay their taxes pawned their watches for a ticket whenever the elder Strauss was playing.

The mechanization of many of Vienna's factories in the early 1800s had created mass unemployment, and as a result there were frequent hunger strikes in the suburbs. Despite all this, Vienna's festive balls continued to draw record crowds—even after the news came from Paris that the Second

Republic had been proclaimed on February 24, 1848. There was talk about the students, whose fraternities had been disbanded by Metternich's police because they supposedly harbored conspiracies of revolutionary thought. It was said that they had found unlikely allies in the liberal burghers and the booksellers, who were going bankrupt owing to censorship. But when the explosion began in Europe's "waltz capital," many Viennese were taken completely by surprise.

The momentous Revolution of 1848 began with a harmless demonstration early on March 13 on the Herrengasse, a distinguished street a short walk from Metternich's chancellery in Ballhausplatz. Students, workers, and burghers met at the Ständehaus to demand freedom of the press, freedom of science, and the resignation of Metternich. At one o'clock, soldiers fired into the crowd, killing thirty people and wounding many more. Sud-

The period between the Congress of Vienna, convened at Schönbrunn in 1814, and the apocalyptic revolution of 1848 is often described as Vienna's golden age. But although Vienna appeared to be serene during the so-called Biedermeier era—as the 1825 street scene above suggests—turmoil lurked just below the surface.

denly the demonstration became a revolt, and later in the afternoon there was a full-scale revolution. By nightfall Metternich had resigned, and the following day he left Vienna. Grillparzer called it "the gayest revolution imaginable . . . the whole population filled the streets all day long."

A new press law was hastily promulgated and armed citizens were permitted to form a national guard. From Vienna, the revolution spread to Budapest, Venice, and Milan, where Austrian soldiers again fired at demonstrators. Unafraid, the Milanese set up barricades and poured boiling water from their windows onto the Austrian soldiers below. It was the beginning of *Cinque Giornate* (The Five Days), Milan and Italy's finest hour. On the fifth day the Austrian commander, General Joseph Radetzky, ordered his troops to retreat to the north. For the first time since 1815, Milan was free of foreign troops.

In May a second wave of the revolution swept Vienna; a new cabinet proclaimed a democratic constitution, and Emperor Ferdinand fled to Innsbruck. The revolution reached Poland, where it was quickly suppressed; Hungary and the Balkans, where Croats, Serbs, Banatians, and Romanians resisted centralist tendencies and formed nationalistic movements; and Prague. There the first Slav Congress was held early in June, attended by representatives of all Slav nations. Significantly, they did not oppose Austria's sovereignty outright but merely demanded liberty, equality, and fraternity in imitation of their French predecessors. Austrian troops then moved into Prague and Prince Alfred Windisch-Graetz, their commander, began shelling the city. Fighting broke out, a state of siege was declared, and the revolt was suppressed. It was not forgotten, however, and after World War I the Czechs were among the first peoples to break away from the Habsburg empire.

In Vienna, meanwhile, the revolution was headed nowhere. The revolutionaries in the polyglot assembly could agree on nothing and fighting eventually broke out between the proestablishment national guard and their enemies, the radical groups. The revolutionaries—students and workers—occupied the railroad station from which Austrian grenadiers were to be sent to Hungary. The grenadiers mutinied, joined the revolutionaries, and stormed the Ministry of War. The war minister was hanged from a lamppost in French revolutionary style; the emperor, who had returned to his capital, made another hasty exit, this time to the Moravian fortress of Olomouc. From there he ordered General Josip Jelačić of Bužima, a Croat nationalist and staunch monarchist, to move his troops against Vienna. He also named Prince Windisch-Graetz, the man who had subdued Prague, supreme commander.

Once more the walls and bastions of Vienna were manned, and people prayed that the relieving army—this time Hungarian—would come. But the Hungarian army was weak, and it was defeated before it could reach Vienna. The revolutionaries fought bravely against the troops of Jelačić, but their cause was foredoomed. The last three days of street fighting were near the gates of the Hofburg, exactly where the worst fighting had taken place during the Turkish siege. On October 31 Windisch-Graetz and his army marched into Vienna, a military dictatorship was proclaimed, and retribution began. The first executions took place in November.

If nothing else, the 1848 revolution had shown the cracks in the foundations of the Danube empire, leading later to wars of national liberation in Hungary and Italy. There great revolutionaries, Kossuth and Garibaldi, became legendary heroes who excited people's imagination. But in Vienna, writes the historian Heinrich Friedjung, "the resistance of the Viennese workers and petit-bourgeois, led by the students, was viewed with skepticism by the better-off section of the population. . . ." And even there the revolution created divisions in many families. One of the most poignant generation gaps occurred in the Strauss family. Johann Strauss the Elder was a member of the establishment; his two oldest sons, Johann and Josef, were revolutionaries. They were young, hated Metternich, and protested against the old order; their weapons were fiddle and bow, their ammunition was melody. The younger Johann Strauss took his musicians to the barricades, where they played his "Revolution March" and the "Marseillaise." "Had he been killed then, he would scarcely have died for the Revolution, but rather for his own intoxication and for beautiful music," writes his biographer, Heinrich Eduard Jacob. Later young Strauss was questioned by the police; although he wasn't arrested he remained suspect at the imperial court, where his appointment as *Hofballmusikdirektor* was delayed until 1863.

Father Strauss, on the other hand, made it quite obvious that he was on the side of the monarchy. On August 31, during the midst of the revolution, he premiered Opus 228 for an audience of high army officers and monarchists, the composition that remains his most famous—the "Radetzky March," in honor of the Austrian commander in Italy. The march, an exciting melody, became the spiritual hymn of the Austrian soldiers. "The Blue Danube," written by Strauss's son and namesake, became the spiritual hymn of all Austrians; and Haydn's "Emperor Hymn" the national anthem. No one was surprised that Austria—musically, at least, a world power—should have three hymns instead of one. Today, at the New Year's concert of the Vienna Philharmonic, the "Radetzky March" is always the first and "The Blue Danube" the second and last encore.

Toward the end of the revolution Emperor Ferdinand had abdicated in favor of his eighteen-year-old nephew, Francis Joseph I. Two years later, the young emperor wrote to his mother, "On Sunday there was a great church parade on the *Glacis*, to show our dear Viennese that troops and guns still exist. . . ." Later, the youthful ruler proclaimed, ". . . disturbing are the effects not of freedom, but of the misuse of freedom. To stop this misuse, and to end the revolution, is Our duty and Our will. . . ." This was absolute monarchy, the old order once more. Paradoxically, Emperor Francis Joseph I, whose regime began with executions and ended with World War I, became one of the greatest and most popular of the Habsburgs. His reign lasted sixty-eight years, an almost uninterrupted succession of political and social disasters and private tragedies. His empire was disintegrating but his age, ironically, became known as Austria's last golden era, and he is now still very much alive in the hearts of the Austrians.

The revolution of 1848, which flickered in March and then burst into full flame in May (opposite), was rather easily quenched in October. Order was rapidly restored, but nothing could be done to contain the ideological fires that now burned in every corner of the Habsburg realm. Wars of national liberation would soon undermine the greatest of all the Danube Basin empires.

5

Vienna's Gay Apocalypse

Der alte Herr, the old Gentleman, is still remembered by older residents of Vienna who saw Francis Joseph I when they were young. And old and young alike are acquainted with the long-dead Habsburg monarch through the uncounted books, operettas, and films based upon his reign of seven decades. When an actor portraying Francis Joseph comes on stage during a performance in Vienna, the audience rises and cheers—a spontaneous reaction that has led perplexed foreigners to conclude that monarchism is widespread in Austria, which is not the case. In fact, the Republic of Austria is now governed by Socialists, traditional enemies of the Habsburgs since workers staged an early May Day parade along the Ringstrasse in 1890. Yet when a somewhat critical portrayal of the emperor was shown a few years ago in the televised version of Joseph Roth's *Radetzkymarsch*, many people, including Socialists, were enraged.

The explanation is complex: Austrians feel instinctively that Francis Joseph personifies the final glorious climax of their country's paradoxically imperial history, one that came at a time when the Danube empire was rapidly disintegrating. In addition the emperor is better understood—and consequently more fully appreciated—now than he was when he was alive. For decades his image was blurred; he was seen either as a stubborn, absolute monarch, fighting to prevent the collapse of his empire, or as a senile father image, given to terminating all public appearances with the same banality: "Es war sehr schön; es hat mich sehr gefreut" (It has been very nice; I have been very pleased). But Francis Joseph was neither the legendary hero created by the operettas nor the antihero presented by antagonistic historians. He had great integrity and dignity, and he was deeply aware of the enormous burden of his exalted office. He was severe in dealing with others but most severe toward himself. He had contempt for corrupt politicians, tolerated no disloyalty, and considered the "Spanish" ceremonial of the court—so called long after the Habsburgs had lost their Spanish possessions—not mere etiquette but the visible expression of a great tradition.

In Francis Joseph's letters to his wife and to the actress Katharina Schratt, he emerges as a lonely, decent man, depressed by a personal fate that made him the symbol of a great, declining power. Hermann Broch, the great Austrian philosopher, calls him "the abstract monarch. . . the epitome of majesty. . . not because he carried a burden of personal misfortune almost as excessive as in a Greek tragedy. . . but because he had come to be, perhaps through his very weaknesses, capable of taking upon himself the awe-inspiring dignity of absolute loneliness. . . . Being the opposite of a people's emperor (*Volkskaiser*) he yet was 'the' Emperor in the eyes of the people." Francis Joseph had austerity and self-respect, not typical Austrian virtues, but he also had Austrian charm and a deep sense of irony, which he revealed to those closest to him, the members of his family and his ministers, but not to many others.

As a young man Francis Joseph had become engaged to a Bavarian princess, one selected by his domineering mother, the Archduchess Sophie. He then fell deeply in love with his fiancée's younger sister, Elizabeth, and he ultimately secured his mother's permission to marry her instead. At the time, Elizabeth was just sixteen, and Francis Joseph was twenty-four. Elizabeth was lovely and popular when she came to Vienna in 1854. It was no secret that she was on bad terms with her formidable mother-in-law, and the people sympathized with her. No one really knows why she became estranged from her husband, a rift that Elizabeth made no effort to hide. Indeed, she often stayed away for months at a time, fox-hunting in England or visiting friends in Hungary. Naturally there was gossip about her mysterious double life, much of it emanating from Viennese who resented her sympathies for Hungary and the Hungarians.

Francis Joseph himself did not become truly popular until after an assassination attempt was made against him in 1853. The Viennese, who admire courage under fire, also admired the emperor's renovation program for the city. When Francis Joseph ascended the throne, the city was still surrounded by old walls that had become anachronistic. Realizing that the superannuated fortifications had outlived their usefulness, he ordered them razed and the moats filled. The top of the old bastion became a beautiful, horseshoe-shaped boulevard surrounding the inner city, its ends resting on the banks of the new Danube Canal, which followed the channel cut eons before by the Roman Danube (see bird's-eye view on following page). Thus Vienna's Ringstrasse, or Ring, as the people called the new boulevard, was not a perfect circle. It was, however, "the visible symbol of the dignity, power and wealth of the empire" that the young emperor had been searching for. He and Elizabeth took an inaugural ride to open it on May 1, 1865. The Ringstrasse later gave its name to a late-nineteenth-century era that was more glittery than golden, and to an eclectic architectural style that fused all earlier Viennese styles.

Gradually great buildings went up at various points along the Ringstrasse and, later, palatial apartment houses were erected on expensive building sites. Unlike Vienna's great baroque palaces, which were paid for by Prince Eugene, various aristocrats, and the Church, the Ringstrasse boom of the 1860's was financed by a few wealthy aristocrats and many nouveau-riche bankers and industrialists seeking status. They paid handsomely for

He was the living symbol of a dying empire; she was his elegant, errant empress. They were Francis Joseph I and Elizabeth of Bavaria (above), last true sovereigns of the Habsburg line.

OVERLEAF: *Under Francis Joseph I's aegis, central Vienna underwent extensive transformation in the mid-1800s. The crumbling bastions encircling the inner city were pulled down and that space given over to a broad new thoroughfare. A sepia drawing executed in 1873 reveals this magnificent, horseshoe-shaped boulevard in all its tree-lined glory. From Karlskirche, at lower left, the arms of the Ringstrasse extend north to the Danube Canal, the river's ancient bed. On the horizon the Danube itself, diverted by the emperor's engineers, cuts a new course.*

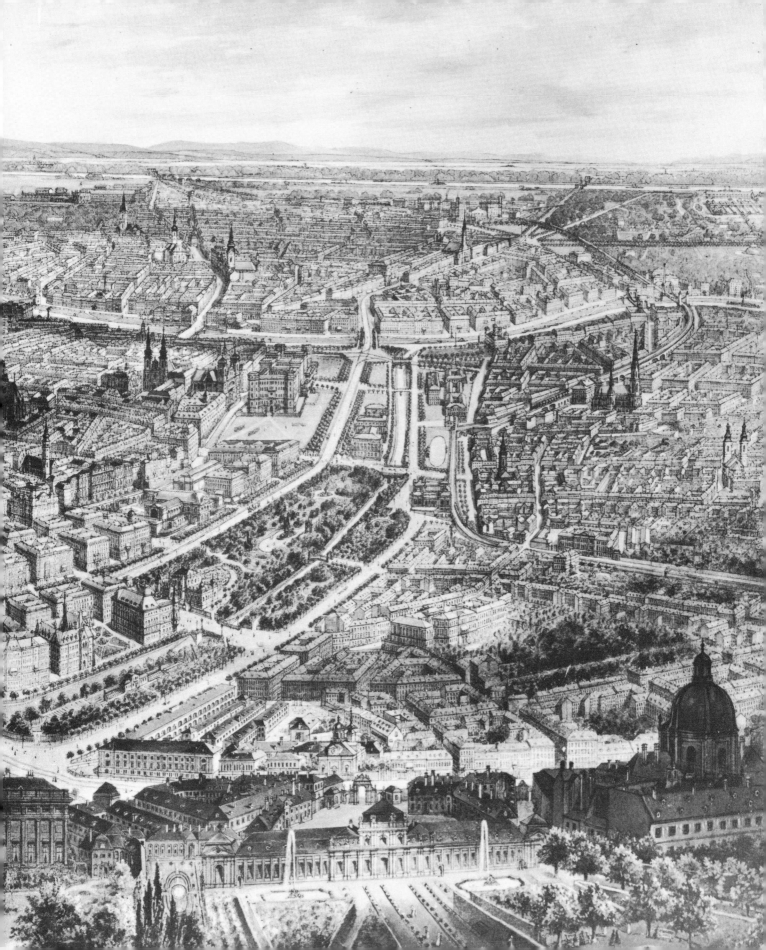

The first important public building to rise along the Ringstrasse was the Court Opera, designed by Siccardsburg and Nüll. Opera-loving Viennese called the new house "music in stone," but Emperor Francis Joseph, who attended the gala opening in May, 1869, pronounced himself displeased with the building's neoclassical façade (above). Only the foyer and the grand staircase of die Oper *(above, near right) survived the Allied bombings of 1945, and to them has been grafted a starkly modern performance hall (above, far right).*

the sites and the buildings, and, moreover, they contributed large sums for laying out the parks and gardens that make the Ringstrasse such an aesthetically successful urban development.

On the finest site of all, where the Ringstrasse crosses Kärntnerstrasse, later the empire's most elegant shopping street, the new Court Opera was built. It was designed by Eduard van der Nüll and August von Siccardsburg in neo-Renaissance style. It is now described as "music in stone," but after its completion *die Oper* was deemed too short. His Majesty was said to be displeased with the completed structure, a judgment that led van der Nüll to commit suicide and Siccardsburg to die of a broken heart two months later. Neither ever saw the finished house.

The Opera may not have pleased purists, being a jumble of styles, but opera fans loved it. Tragically, the Americans mistakenly bombed the structure in the final days of World War II; only the foyer and grand staircase with Moritz von Schwind's poetic reproductions from *The Magic Flute* have survived—although a timeless and unobtrusive theater has been built behind the preserved façade.

The next two buildings finished along the new Ringstrasse in the later nineteenth century were the court museums. The Museum for the History of Art (Kunsthistorisches) houses treasures collected by the Habsburgs from their vast dominions. These include fifteenth-century Flemish master-

pieces, sixteenth-century German works, canvases executed by the great Italian masters—Bellini, Giorgione, Lotto, Palma Vecchio, Titian, Tintoretto—and some superb paintings by Rembrandt and Velázquez. The museum's great pride is its Pieter Brueghel collection, which represents nearly half of all the artist's known paintings. In all, the collection reflects the exquisite taste of the Habsburgs, and especially of those who acquired the best works, Archduke Leopold William and Emperor Rudolf II.

Paired with the Kunsthistoriches is the Museum for Natural History (Naturhistorisches). Gottfried Semper designed both museums in neo-Renaissance style, with a formal garden between them and a statue of Empress Maria Theresa, surrounded by her field marshals, in the middle. Semper also planned an imperial forum that would link the museums by triumphal arches to two new wings of the Hofburg, directly across the Ringstrasse. Only one wing was built, however, and a beautiful garden was laid out in lieu of the other.

Next to the museums, Danish architect Theophil Hansen built the new House of Parliament in neo-Hellenistic style. (He had earlier built the neo-Renaissance Musikverein, possibly the world's most acoustically perfect concert hall.) Several blocks distant is Vienna's neo-Gothic city hall, which looks like a bad copy of Gothic town halls in Belgium. Across from it is the neo-Renaissance Burgtheater, so criticized upon its completion that it had

to be completely redone. Not surprisingly, this jumble of classically derived styles was bitterly criticized by younger artists, who denounced the Ring-strasse style as pretentious and pathetic. What they failed to note was that these buildings, in combination with the Ring's large parks, formal gardens, and open spaces, create a harmonious baroque synthesis: imposing public buildings and noble, though faintly run-down, apartment houses, linden trees along the Ringstrasse, and beyond them the rounded hills of the Wie-nerwald. Suddenly, one no longer cares about the style because the ensemble is beautiful. Reflecting the new Vienna of Francis Joseph, the Ring-strasse magnificently concealed its manifold tragedies.

In 1866 the Iron Chancellor of Prussia, Otto von Bismarck, created a fateful alliance with France and the new kingdom of Italy and attacked Austria. The Austrians halted the Italians, but they never recovered from the disastrous defeat by Prussia at Königgrätz. With the Prussians preparing to cross the Danube at Pressburg, the citizens of Vienna once again prepared to flee. The imperial treasury chests and gold reserves were hastily evacuated, but Francis Joseph, thirty-six, failed to observe a Habsburg tradition, declaring he would leave Vienna only "when military events made it imperative." Such events never occurred, but in the subsequent Treaty of Prague Austria was forced to cede Venetia, its last possession in Italy, to France. Austria's humiliating defeat also encouraged widespread rebellion in Hungary, and Vienna managed to keep Hungary in the empire only by establishing the principle of dualism. Henceforth, it was decreed, the Habsburg monarchy would be called Austria-Hungary, the emperor of Austria would be crowned in Budapest as king of Hungary, and the Hungarians would be given considerable autonomy. This Compromise of 1867 infuriated the Slavs in Bohemia, Moravia, Silesia, and Galicia, who also demanded autonomy. The handwriting was on the wall, but no one in Vienna seemed to want to see it.

After the 1866 defeat by the Prussians, the mood in the normally buoyant waltz city along the Danube was momentarily subdued. To lift Vienna from this despond, the greatest waltz composer wrote his best-known masterpiece, one that gave the people new hope again—and, incidentally, made the Danube the most popular river on earth. Johann Strauss, forty-two and already famous, was asked by Johann Herbeck, who would later become director of the Court Opera, to write a new waltz for the carnival concert of the Vienna Men's Choral Society. Strauss pointedly informed Herbeck this was no time to write a new waltz; people were clearly too depressed to respond to a lighthearted tune. Never mind, said Herbeck, give the people something to be cheerful about.

As he considered Herbeck's request, Strauss remembered a poem by Karl Isidor Beck: a love song to Vienna—or to a woman in Vienna—that ended with the words, "an der Donau, an der schönen blauen Donau" (on the Danube, on the beautiful blue Danube). In his childhood, Strauss had lived in the Leopoldstadt district near the Danube and had watched the boatmen dancing and the musicians playing. To him the river had often appeared gray or greenish, and occasionally silver in the moonlight, but

The Court Opera was but the first gem in the Ringstrasse diadem, and by the time Vienna's late-nineteenth-century building boom abated "the Ring" had been girdled with magnificent public and private buildings. These included the court museums, neo-Renaissance structures linked by a formal garden; and the new House of Parliament (opposite), which a contemporary writer called "a triumph of neo-Hellenism."

Vienna was already regarded as the waltz capital of Europe—and Johann Strauss the Younger was already recognized as a past master of the form—when he composed the simple melody shown below. The choral society for whom Strauss created "The Blue Danube" pronounced the work unsingable, but it soon won the hearts of all Vienna. Unofficial theme song of both river and city, it was played everywhere—even at court balls such as the one at near right, attended by the doughty Francis Joseph himself. And when Strauss died in 1899, the citizens of Vienna erected an appropriately graceful and lighthearted memorial (far right) in his honor.

almost never blue. Yet the poet's imagination caught the composer's genius, spurring Strauss to write a wonderfully simple, thirty-two-bar waltz melody based on a single motif, the D-major triad.

People have speculated endlessly about "The Blue Danube" waltz with its impressionistic tremolo introduction of the strings, "the sound of the river." Strauss, who never talked about his music, may or may not have consciously tried to evoke the mood of the Danube, but for the world at large his music epitomized the very heartbeat of Vienna. The apparently eternal appeal of the century-old waltz is its identification with all that people everywhere think is Vienna. Without being sentimental, the *Donauwalzer* encourages genuine sentiment. The Viennese critic Eduard Hanslick called it "a patriotic folk song, a peaceful 'Marseillaise.' "

The great waltz actually has a rather ironic history. For one thing, it wasn't written for orchestra but for the members of Herbeck's choral

society. One of those members, Joseph Weyl, a police official, wrote the strange text that begins:

Wiener, seid froh!	Vienna, be gay!
Oho! Wieso?	And why, pray?
Ein Schimmer des Lichts—	A glimmer of light—
Wir sehn noch nichts!	With us, it's night!
Der Fasching ist da!	Carnival is here!
Ah so, na na!	Oh yes, well then!

Trite and somewhat silly when read aloud, Weyl's lyrics sounded even sillier when sung alternately by tenor and bass choruses. Members of the society promptly declared the new work "idiotic, unsingable, unmelodious." Small wonder, then, that the world's first performance, in Vienna on February 13, 1867, was no success. The waltz was a smash hit in Paris, however, when Strauss himself conducted it at that year's Paris Exposition.

OVERLEAF: *Blue only in the imaginations of poets and expatriate Viennese, the Danube at Vienna is a gray sheet, the broad gateway to Eastern Europe.*

The French critics, more perceptive than their Viennese colleagues, called it "the waltz of waltzes." Strauss had done the impossible: he had made the depressed Viennese happy, and he had painted the Danube blue.

On May 1, 1873, the great Vienna Exhibition was opened in the presence of Emperor Francis Joseph, Empress Elizabeth, Crown Prince Rudolf, and rulers from all parts of Europe who had come to see the fair that was billed as "five times the area of the former Paris Fair." For the first time since the Congress of Vienna in 1815, Vienna was again the capital of Europe—for exactly one week. On Vienna's Black Friday—May 9, eight days after the exhibition opened—the Viennese Stock Exchange crash ruined local and foreign speculators, wiped out many of the nouveaux riches, and created a new wave of anti-Semitism despite the fact that many Jews were financially ruined too. The shock waves of this disaster were felt all over Europe and in the Americas as well. The local papers reported that Vienna's famed dance halls were deserted and that there was a wave of suicides. As a band passed the Stock Exchange playing "The Blue Danube," a bystander with a macabre sense of humor yelled, "Go ahead, look at your damn blue Danube, it's full of dead bodies!"

Within a matter of weeks, however, Strauss was to write a beautiful new waltz, "Wiener Blut," the Viennese were to recover their perpetual optimism, and the dance halls were to fill once again. Soon Strauss was working on his masterpiece, *Die Fledermaus*, the greatest operetta of all. Its premiere, eleven months after the crash, was a glorious event—and it was followed, in 1879, by the silver wedding anniversary of Francis Joseph and Elizabeth, the finest hour of the Ringstrasse. Hans Makart, the painter from Salzburg whose name became synonymous with sensuous decadence and extravagant kitsch, produced a post-baroque supershow, an enormous pageant that moved slowly down the Ringstrasse to the Imperial Palace, where Their Majesties watched the improbable procession of floats, riders, music bands, and costumed guilds with bemusement. Makart himself led the parade riding on a white charger. At one point the horse almost threw him, and many people were sorry that it had not, for they detested Makart for his indiscreet love affairs and vulgar exhibitionism. It was, for example, a populor parlor games to guess the identity of the allegorical nudes in his monumental paintings; they always looked strikingly similar to prominent actresses and society women.

A long overdue and altogether healthy reaction against Ringstrasse kitsch occurred in 1897 when a group of young artists seceded from the Künstlerhaus, the conservative art establishment. The secessionists moved into a modest building in the nearby Getreidemarkt, where they published an avant-garde magazine called *Ver Sacrum* (Sacred Spring). Their aim was nothing less than "to rejuvenate the living style of a dying city," and for several years Vienna became the breeding ground and laboratory of what was later known as modern art. Among the prominent secessionists were the architect Otto Wagner; Joseph Hoffmann, founder of the renowned *Wiener Werkstätte*; and the painters Gustav Klimt and his immensely gifted colleague Egon Schiele, who died in 1918 at the age of twenty-eight.

Ten years after their silver wedding anniversary, Francis Joseph and Elizabeth suffered a terrible ordeal. In the early morning hours of January 30, 1889, they were informed that their only son, Crown Prince Rudolf, had shot Mary Vetsera, a seventeen-year-old girl from a rich Viennese family, and then shot himself in the second-floor bedroom of his hunting lodge at Mayerling, in the Wienerwald. The drama of Mayerling has fascinated the Viennese for generations, but the mystery that once surrounded this double tragedy largely evaporated in 1955 when the records of Baron Krauss, Vienna's police chief at the time, were published in facsimile. The records revealed that after the corpses were discovered, Krauss ordered that the body of Mary Vetsera be removed from Mayerling by coach. For her final ride she was propped up in her seat, made to look as though she were alive, and supported by her uncles, the brothers Baltazzi. That very night she was furtively buried in the secluded Cistercian Abbey of Heiligenkreuz.

The first published reports of the incident indicated that Rudolf had died of a heart attack. Later, disregarding the urgent advice of his minis-

To mark the silver wedding anniversary of Francis Joseph and his peripatetic empress, Elizabeth, the Viennese staged a day-long pageant that circled the Ringstrasse and terminated in front of the Hofburg. A contemporary water-color shows the emperor emerging from that palace in a closed coach drawn by eight prancing Lipizzaner stallions.

was published in Vienna in 1899. By that time he had already risen to the rank of *Privatdocent* (university lecturer), but despite his growing reputation he had to wait until 1902 to be made professor *extraordinarius*, unsalaried—not because he was a Jew, as is often believed, but owing to intrigues in high bureaucratic circles. In the interim the university's professorial college proposed Freud's promotion on several occasions, but bureaucrats at the Ministry of Education always turned down the college's recommendation on "budgetary" grounds.

Freud's belated appointment brought a temporary truce in the ongoing war between Vienna's intelligentsia and her bureaucracy, but the battle was soon joined again over other issues. Metternich, himself a superbureaucrat, once shrewdly observed that Austria was "not ruled but administered." And Victor Adler, turn-of-the-century leader of the Social-Democratic party, labeled Viennese bureaucracy a state within the state, "despotism mitigated by muddle." The definition is still valid, for Austria's powerful bureaucracy, although no longer *kaiserlich und königlich*, "imperial and royal," has survived the Habsburg monarchy and all later regimes and now administers the republic.

Because its clientele included the city's leading critics, philosophers, and poets, Vienna's legendary Café Griensteidl (below) offered patrons dozens of different newspapers, an encyclopedia, and an unlimited supply of writing paper. Claiming that they could create nowhere else, Griensteidl habitués would arrive each afternoon, order "Nothing, as usual," and settle down to their work.

Even before the secessionist artists rebelled against the pretentious decay of the Ringstrasse style, some young writers and critics had formed the Jung Wien (Young Vienna) group and begun meeting at the Griensteidl, a literary café near the Hofburg. There poets and satirists, essayists and hangers-on would talk endlessly, always about Vienna. The coffeehouse itself was not a Viennese invention—long before double agent Koltschitzky opened his establishment after the second siege there had been celebrated cafés in Constantinople, Oxford, London, and Venice—but the Viennese variety became a local phenomenon of great social importance. Vienna's coffeehouses were long a cradle of literature, a focus of scientific thought, and a breeding ground of revolutions. During the *Vormärz* days, Neuner's Café, where all fixtures were made of pure silver, was considered especially suspect by the police, who carefully watched the writers and politicians who gathered there. Metternich's secret agents always raided the coffeehouses first when there was trouble, and Hitler's Gestapo later did the same. The Café Griensteidl had mountains of newspapers, a complete set of encyclopedias, and foolscap for writers who claimed they could only create there. One did not even have to order. "The Herr Doktor is having nothing, as usual," the headwaiter would tell the underwaiter.

Griensteidl, home of neo-romanticism and impressionism, closed in 1897—perhaps too many guests had ordered "nothing, as usual"—and its clientele moved to the nearby Café Central, which was said to be "not a coffeehouse but a *Weltanschauung*, a refuge from *Angst*." Among its habitués were *Angst*-expert Sigmund Freud, Mayor Karl Lueger, and his arch-rival, Victor Adler. In the rear, gathered Professor Tomáš G. Masaryk and Karel Kramář, who were said to manufacture "imperial-royal high treason against the Monarchy." Masaryk later became the first president of Czechoslovakia. Kramář was sentenced for treason; pardoned, he became Czechoslovakia's first prime minister. In the chessroom a Russian émigré named Bronstein played game after game with Vienna's grand masters. Later, under the name of Leon Trotsky, he was to mastermind the overthrow of the Romanov dynasty. A doubtlessly apocryphal story claims that Count Czernin, Austria's foreign minister, upon being told of the October Revolution in Russia, exclaimed, "Who made it? Could it be Herr Bronstein from the Café Central?"

The *Kaffeehaus* is to the Viennese what the club is to the Londoners. Stefan Zweig, the noted novelist, called it "our best educational establishment for all that is new." Anyone could join who had the money for a cup of coffee—or a friend willing to pay for him. As a result, the coffeehouse soon spread to the faraway corners of the Danube empire. There it was said to have a "subtly colonizing influence," although purists claimed that the cafés in such places as Kraków and Trieste, Budapest and Innsbruck were mere imitations and that the original, found only in Vienna, offered a unique juxtaposition of hospitality and living space, companionship and seclusion, good talk and silence, tolerance and conspiracy.

When all is said and done, it is not for cafés, literature, science, or architecture, however, that Vienna will be remembered, but for music. Vienna

Above all else, nineteenth-century Vienna was a city of music. There Mozart, Haydn, Beethoven, and a host of lesser talents lived and worked, and there music was unquestionably the best loved of all the arts. Beethoven's Fidelio *received its premiere at the Theatre-an-der-Wien (above) in 1805. That hymn to love and freedom was to be played with renewed feeling in 1955 when the Soviets withdrew from Vienna.*

is the birthplace of classical, romantic, and modern music—and the melodies created there will live long after the city's baroque palaces have become noble ruins. Since the dawn of history, the peoples who moved through the Danube Basin have contributed their folk songs and dance melodies to the general store. The result is that while the Germans consider themselves "the nation of poets and thinkers," the Austrians are known as "the nation of fiddlers and dancers."

Music was a way of life in the Danube region, and although the Habsburgs occasionally scrimped on their palaces, they were never niggardly when it came to music and opera. Many members of the ruling family played musical instruments, and some, such as Leopold I, were able composers. Joseph II always spent an hour playing music after dinner, and Joseph's brother, the Archduke Maximilian, often conducted in the Schönbrunn. Francis I played first violin with his string quartet at Castle Persenbeug, and on quiet evenings the boatmen on the Danube below could hear the soft strains of the music.

Vienna certainly had no claim to early music, which was created first in Greece and Byzantium, and later in Italy, Burgundy, England, and elsewhere. Indeed, much great music had already been composed by the time the classical era began in Vienna. The somewhat arbitrary but widely accepted date for the beginning of this era is October 5, 1762, the Viennese premiere of Christoph Willibald von Gluck's *Orfeo ed Euridice*, the first modern musical drama. During the next 150 years, Gluck, Haydn, Mozart, Beethoven, and Schubert worked in Vienna; after them came Brahms, Bruckner, Mahler, Johann Strauss, and Richard Strauss, and, in our own century, Schönberg, Berg, and Webern. Of these world-renowned musicians, only Schubert and Johann Strauss were actually born in Vienna. The other composers all migrated there, attracted by the musical climate. Many stayed forever, "bewitched," as Leopold Mozart, the composer's father, put it, by the city's unique aura.

Coincidentally, 1762 was also the year that Father Mozart brought his two children and a small piano down the Danube from Linz to Vienna on the "water-ordinary," or mailboat. At the Danube customshouse the six-year-old Wolfgang Amadeus amused officials by playing a minuet on his small fiddle, and they permitted his piano to be taken into town without payment of the usual toll fee. Later the Danube boatmen who shipped timber on the Alpine tributaries and down the Danube also brought their dancing melodies to Vienna. The origins of the waltz may have been in Bavaria, the Tyrol, and other mountain regions, but the transformation of the robust *Laendler* of the boatmen into the sensuous, romantic waltzes is a wholly Viennese phenomenon. The most popular, most durable dance of the Western world was indisputably created between the Danube and the hills of the Wienerwald.

No other city on earth has so many locales associated with great music. Not far from the small Heuriger Garden in Grinzing, where Schubert and his friends spent afternoons, Beethoven would walk, alone and brooding. He particularly loved a narrow path that meandered toward Kahlenberg;

Turn-of-the-century Vienna was a city suffused with waltz melodies and buoyed by false confidence. In retrospect this period would be known as "Vienna's gay apocalypse," and it is that aura of spurious serenity that pervades this 1895 panorama of an open-air vegetable market on the banks of the Danube Canal.

there, he informed his friend Anton Schindler, he had composed the *Pastoral* Symphony. Mozart wrote the divine *Figaro* on the second floor of the Camesina House, and Haydn completed both *The Creation* and *The Seasons* at 19 Haydngasse, now the Haydn Museum. From his home in Karlsgasse, Brahms could see Karlskirche and the small house where Schubert had lived, leading the great composer to observe, "With every step we are treading on classical soil!" The Prater, a large park and amusement ground near the Danube, has been associated with romance and waltz music ever since Robert Stolz wrote "Im Prater blüh'n wieder die Bäume" ("It's blossom time again in the Prater"). Here and elsewhere, Vienna's *genius loci* remains strong.

This is not to say that the great composers were always fully appreciated in Vienna. Mozart, for instance, was cheered in Prague when he conducted *Figaro*, but was not well received in Vienna, where *Figaro* was dropped in favor of *Una cosa rara* by Vicente Martin y Soler, a work now mercifully forgotten. And Schubert was never really accepted in Europe's musical capital except by a small circle of friends. Toward the end of his life, Beethoven noted of Schubert: "Truly he has the divine spark." But Schubert never dared speak to Beethoven when they met in the street. Later, Wagner was to be admired by a few and ridiculed by many, and Gustav Mahler was to be more highly thought of as director of the Court Opera than as a composer. When Mahler conducted his Fourth Symphony at the Musikverein, the mood was so hostile that fellow conductor Bruno Walter, who was in the audience, feared there might be a fight between a few admirers and the rest of the audience. The works of Arnold Schönberg were performed in his native city only a few years ago, long after they had been heard elsewhere. The Viennese are emotional and conservative listeners, for many of whom music ended with Brahms and Bruckner.

Much great music in Vienna was written for emperors, noblemen, and the upper classes, but the Viennese operetta, one of the city's durable exports, was written for the burghers, the common people. The operetta was not invented in Vienna but in Paris, where Jacques Offenbach's *La Belle Héléne* was first performed in 1864. That year, however, Offenbach came to Vienna, where he casually told Johann Strauss, "You ought to write operettas." Strauss, following this advice, wrote the finest operetta of all, *Die Fledermaus*, in 1874. He did so at a particularly opportune moment, for between 1860 and 1890, while the populations of Paris and London were increasing by 60 percent, Vienna's had jumped by 259 percent as immigrants from the provinces of the Danube empire—Bohemia, Moravia, Hungary, Serbia, Italy—poured into Vienna. By 1910, Vienna had two million inhabitants, and these new Viennese, many of them lower class, were especially attracted by the cosmopolitan features of the operetta. The story usually took place in one of the provinces, and the music would contain a Bohemian polka, a Polish mazurka, a Hungarian czardas—unified by a Viennese waltz.

The short, happy life of the Viennese operetta lasted only from 1874 until 1905, the year that Franz Lehár's *The Merry Widow* was performed

at the venerable Theater an der Wien. Of the vast production of operettas, about a dozen by Strauss, Lehár, Karl Millöcker, Emmerich Kálmán, and Oskar Straus have survived. In Vienna, as in Paris, the operetta died with the monarchy. In the 1880s, six theaters performed operettas; today only the Volksoper specializes in the dying genre. The music may still sound good, but the librettos often seem silly and the jokes passé.

In the two or three decades preceding World War I, the rich intellectual and artistic life of the capital no longer concealed the widening cracks in the structure of the Habsburg empire. The men near the center of power saw the fissures but did little about them, attempting instead to save their own careers. Archduke Francis Ferdinand, a nephew of Francis Joseph who had become heir to the throne after Rudolf's death, was a conservative with the ambitions of a despot; Professor Freud might have called him a neurotic. The archduke was said to have "cool and formal relations" with the emperor, despite the fact that Francis Joseph forgave him for marrying Sophie, duchess of Hohenberg, a former lady-in-waiting of middling station. Although Francis Ferdinand had to renounce his heirs' right to succeed to the Habsburg throne, his marriage to Sophie was a happy one. He was said to be a champion of the Slavs, wanting to give them a greater share in the government after he came to power.

"I don't want war," Francis Joseph told his ministers, "I have always been unlucky in wars." And for almost a decade the aged emperor was able to hold Austria's pro-war faction in check. Then, in late June of 1914, the emperor's heir, Archduke Francis Ferdinand, and the latter's young wife, Sophie (above), made their fateful trip to Sarajevo, restive capital of the recently annexed state of Bosnia. There, on a street named for the emperor, they were cut down by an assassin—and the cataclysm that Francis Joseph had feared for so long became an inevitability.

After the annexation of Bosnia and Herzegovina in 1908, a powerful group at the court favored a more aggressive policy in the Balkans. This, it was seriously claimed, might lead to "a healthy, invigorating war" that would be "surgery needed to restore the recovery of the ailing Habsburg empire." The emperor's chief of staff, General Conrad von Hötzendorf, even suggested a preventive war against Italy, which then happened to be Austria's nominal ally. The war party continued to gain strength at court in the early 1900s despite the octogenarian emperor's protests. "I don't want war," Francis Joseph said in 1912. "I've always been unlucky in wars—we'd win, but we'd lose provinces." Adamant in opposition, War Minister Krobatin insisted that starting a war was the only way to solve Austria's internal problems. Joseph Redlich, a member of the government and later a prominent historian, wrote in 1913: "That ancient man on the throne, and the weaklings around him, do not see that only the sword can still save Austria. Insurrection is lying in ambush in Dalmatia, Croatia and Bosnia! Sometimes I blame myself for not speaking up for war energetically."

In that same year a major depression created high levels of unemployment and produced numerous bankruptcies. In May, Colonel Redl of the Austrian general staff was arrested and charged with conveying army mobilization plans to the Russians, who found out about his homosexuality and had blackmailed him. The *affaire* Redl is still remembered in books and films for its dramatic end, which came when two fellow officers left a loaded revolver in Redl's room at the Hotel Klomser and then patiently waited in front of the hotel entrance until they heard a shot. The affair convinced partisans of a preventive war that there was little time left.

Then, at three minutes past eleven, on the morning of June 28, 1914, Archduke Francis Ferdinand and his wife were shot dead on Francis Joseph Street in Sarajevo, the capital of Bosnia, by a Serbian nationalist named Gavrilo Princip. The shots at Sarajevo were exactly what many people in Vienna had been waiting for. Francis Joseph I, who at eighty-four had forgotten nothing but had learned nothing, listened to his generals and members of the war party, as he had done before. This time the old man sadly concluded, "If the monarchy must go down, it shall at least, go down decently. . . ." Austria would mobilize, which meant that Russia and Germany would also mobilize. And thus World War I was ignited. Francis Joseph did not live to see the horrifying consequences of his actions: twenty million casualties, a continent in ruins—and peace treaties that contained the seeds of another, even more terrible conflict.

According to at least one contemporary observer, Francis Joseph "reigned in reality only until the death of Johann Strauss" in 1899. In actuality, of course, the Old Gentleman lingered on until 1916. By that time the entire Danube Basin had been engulfed in the most destructive war in its history. For the citizens of Belgrade, the war began on July 28, 1914, when the four-inch guns of Austria's Danube flotilla began shelling the Yugoslav capital (left).

6

Between World Wars

*T*he centrifugal forces of nationalism and social revolution that broke up the Habsburg empire at the end of World War I were not contained by the peace treaties of 1919, written under the idealistic influence of President Woodrow Wilson. During the war, tens of thousands of Czechs, Poles, Serbs, and Slovenes had committed acts of sabotage and espionage against Austria-Hungary, the state to which they still owed technical loyalty. Czechs took off their Austrian uniforms, deserted to the Russians, and later formed separate legions, fighting against their homeland. Many Serbs and Transylvanian Romanians also deserted.

During the war years a subtle form of sabotage known as Schweikism developed in Bohemia and Moravia. This movement took its name from *The Good Soldier Schweik*, the fictional masterpiece of Jaroslav Hašek, a Czech writer often compared to Rabelais, Cervantes, and Swift. The Good Soldier was soon recognized as a universal type—a naïve but cunning little man who generates confusion by following orders verbatim and who reduces pompous bureaucrats and military superiors to absurdity by taking them quite seriously. He tries to do everything right and invariably does everything wrong.

At the end of World War I, many men of goodwill said that only the principle of self-determination could create a new and better Europe. Then, with the resignation of Charles I (son of Archduke Francis Ferdinand) on November 12, 1918, the 645-year-old Habsburg dynasty came to a sudden, anticlimactic end, and the Habsburgs' Danube empire broke up into the successor states of Hungary, Czechoslovakia, Yugoslavia, Poland, Romania (somewhat enlarged by the dissection of the empire), and the small republic of Austria. Vienna, once the capital of a monarchy embracing fifty million people, now ruled a country of a mere seven million.

Politically, the nations were free at last, and many people anticipated a bright and better future. Economically, the breakup of the Danube empire was a tragedy, later admitted by many of those who had helped to engineer it. In this regard, one example suffices: toward the end of the nineteenth century the Habsburg monarchy had built railroads running from Vienna to all parts of its far-flung empire. Now the successor states found themselves at the nether end of an absurd communications network that fed into Vienna, a hungry, bankrupt capital cut off from its hinterland.

All successor states had enormous problems, but Austria's situation was least tenable of all. No one who lived through the chaotic postwar years in Vienna wants to remember them. Indeed, there are people living in Vienna who have lost their savings several times over in their lives: after World War I, when the monarchy's war bonds became worthless scraps of paper; during the worldwide depression that began in Vienna in 1931 with the collapse of a leading bank, the Creditanstalt; and both during and after World War II. In the 1920s the Viennese often remembered the sarcastic aphorism of the great playwright Nestroy: "The noblest nation is resignation." Only a people trained by history in the art of survival could have managed to live through this nightmare of hunger and cold, financial chaos and astronomical inflation. During the worst of it, a streetcar ride cost millions of schillings, prices were changed in the shops every ten minutes, and diners in restaurants asked to pay when they ordered—for fear the price might go up by the time they had been served. Only black-marketeers were able to survive comfortably.

Once more, and perhaps for the last time, Vienna enjoyed a brilliant intellectual life; for a while it was *the* literary city of the German-speaking countries. A visitor to Vienna in the middle 1920s might have seen Sigmund Freud, Arthur Schnitzler, the great director Max Reinhardt (who somehow found money to rebuild the beautiful Josefstadt Theater), the cultural historian Egon Friedell, the gifted novelist Ödön von Horváth, the satirist Karl Kraus, great novelists and great musicians. Paradoxically, the theater again dominated cultural life, as always in times of disaster. The make-believe of the stage gave an illusion of happiness and a few hours of escape; and anyway an opera ticket cost less than a few slices of sausage. Suddenly there were dozens of new banks, and when the banks went bankrupt their premises were often transformed into coffeehouses. There were said to be at least twelve hundred of the latter, but naturally no one ever bothered to count them.

Politically, things went from bad to worse. In 1920 the Social Democrats abandoned their efforts to maintain an uneasy coalition government, and the Catholic People's party established one-party rule. But the unhappy division of Black and Red remained: the federal chancellor was traditionally a Black (Catholic), the federal president was often a Red (Socialist). Then, in 1934, Vienna lived through five terrible days of civil war as Chancellor Engelbert Dollfuss dissolved all political parties except his own and ordered the army to shell the homes of Austrian workers where Socialist leaders had gathered. By that time one-party rule had become synonymous with dictatorship. For years thereafter the pockmarked façades of the apartment blocks shelled by Dollfuss's men were left as a memento of a trauma that has never really faded from the Austrian consciousness.

A few months later, shortly after parliament was dissolved, Dollfuss was murdered by two members of the then-illegal Nazi party—scarcely a year

Bankrupt, hungry, and cold, the desperate citizens of Vienna survived the first winter after the war by logging over the Vienna Woods (above) and using that cordwood to heat their homes.

after Adolf Hitler, an obscure, Austrian artist *manqué* from Braunau am Inn, a tributary of the Danube, had come to power in Germany. Dollfuss's successor, Kurt von Schuschnigg, bravely resisted the mounting pressure for union coming from Germany, where Hitler had proclaimed that he would bring Austria "home" into the Third Reich.

Adolf Hitler had often walked in Linz, where he went to school, and in Vienna, where he sold postcards along the Danube. He had megalomaniacal dreams of a new Danubian empire, one much larger than the Habsburgs had ever dreamed of. The Third Reich would embrace all German-speaking people in Europe and would reach from the North Sea to the Black Sea, with its center in the old Danube Basin. In retrospect, Hitler's schedule looks diabolical but also highly ingenious: the breaking of the chains of Versailles and his proclaiming the disarmament clause null and void in 1935; the reoccupation of the demilitarized Rhineland in 1936; and the playing off of France against Britain over the civil war in Spain. Finally, in March, 1938, German troops occupied Austria. Seemingly hypnotized, the Western powers did nothing to help Austria, and the Führer was enthusiastically welcomed to Vienna by a considerable part of the populace. The

For Adolph Hitler, Anschluss with Austria in March, 1938, was a special sort of triumph, as the photograph below suggests. The German dictator had been born in Upper Austria and had begun his career as an architect's assistant in Vienna. Before emigrating to Munich in 1912, the young draftsman executed a number of sketches of the capital of the Habsburg empire. Hitler's agents were later to ferret out and destroy most of these works, but a handful have survived. These include the sketch of Karlskirche opposite, above, and the view of Parliament below it.

newsreels of Hitler's triumphal arrival in the capital still exist, and they remain a source of acute embarrassment to a great many people. The new chancellor, Artur von Seyss-Inquart, proclaimed *Anschluss*, the political union of Germany and Austria that was subsequently ratified by an overwhelming majority of Austria's citizens. By the time they realized how foolish they had been, it was too late: Austrians in German uniforms were fighting the Führer's battles in World War II.

Of all the successor states, the case of Czechoslovakia is the most tragic. Tomáš Masaryk won an uphill fight in 1918 for the self-determination and political independence of his nation, which for three hundred years had been dominated by the Habsburgs. President Wilson had promised "to make the world safe for democracy," and Czechoslovakia was the only state in Central Europe where American-style democracy was, for a time, a fact and not merely a wishful dream.

Masaryk's fine idea was to make his country, whose constitution was modeled on the American Constitution, a Central-European Switzerland where Czechs and Slovaks, Germans and Jews, Hungarians and Ruthenians, and other minorities could live side by side in peace and prosperity. It

Its journey to the sea slightly more than a third over, the sunstruck Danube (left) sweeps past Vienna and glides through the so-called Hungarian Gate near Bratislava in Czechoslovakia. Beyond this point, forests give way to treeless flatlands, and tourism to commerce. This is the true Danube, the vital lifeline of Eastern Europe. Livestock are watered along its banks, produce moves along its broad course, and dams tap its hydroelectric potential. For nine ice-free months each year, commercial traffic teems on this "dustless highway" across the face of Eastern Europe.

For hundreds of miles at a stretch the middle Danube rolls across trackless grasslands whose features are as timeless as the river's own. But the twentieth century has left its impress upon the landscape—as, since World War II, entire cities (above) have risen along the Danube's flanks.

was an audacious experiment and one that worked well until the Great Depression hit Central Europe.

Masaryk was a humanist and philosopher, a statesman and citizen of the world; few countries ever permitted themselves the luxury of such a leader, or were lucky enough to find one. As a young man, Masaryk wrote a scholarly dissertation proving that the manuscripts of Zelená Hora and Králový Dvur, epic songs about the foundation of Prague, had been forged—and for many years Czech nationalists hated him for deflating a cherished legend. Later he again made himself unpopular by condemning the trial of Leopold Hilsner, an impoverished Jew accused of the ritual murder of a Czech girl; Hilsner's innocence was subsequently proved. Fittingly, Masaryk took as his motto, when he became first president, the slogan of Jan Hus, *Pravda Vítezí*—"Truth Prevails."

In Prague—and only there—Czech, German, and Jewish writers lived side by side during the years of Masaryk's republic, until his death in 1937. German poet Rainer Marie Rilke, who sensed the rhythm of the Czech language so well that he used the words of the Czech national anthem in one of his German-language poems, wrote poetry about Jan Hus. There too Max Brod, Franz Kafka's closest friend, translated Leoš Janáček's opera *Jenufa* into German, making the great Moravian composer famous in his sixties, at a time when even Czech critics had not yet discovered him. And Franz Werfel, who wrote beautiful poetry in Prague before he went to Vienna, married the widow of Gustav Mahler and lent support to the Catholic government. And, finally, it was in Prague that Franz Kafka, a Jew who wrote crystal-clear German sentences, fell deeply in love with Milena Jesenská, a gifted Czech writer who died in a German concentration camp.

Living in a linguistic ghetto, the German-language poets of Prague set their standards by the finest examples, Goethe and Heine. Few writers have ever approached the sublime beauty of the language written by Rilke,

Werfel, and Kafka; even in Vienna and Berlin it was admitted that the best German was being written in Prague. Czech writers too had their great renaissance. Masaryk went almost every Friday night to the villa of the fine writers Karel and Josef Čapek. The president felt much at home there, more than in his splendid official residence in Hradčany Castle. Karel Čapek, in his mysteries, utopias, and moralities, showed a remarkable sense of prophecy that was not unlike Kafka's.

Masaryk's republic did not—perhaps could not—last. It was beautifully conceived, but it incorporated too many restless minorities. The Slovaks demanded autonomy, which the Czechs refused to grant them; and although political liberty and progressive social institutions existed, the country's geographic and geopolitical location between Germany and Russia proved fateful—confirming Bismarck's observation that "He who holds Bohemia holds Europe." In the early years of Nazi Germany, Czechoslovakia remained a democratic country, giving refuge to victims of Nazism from both Germany and Austria. No wonder, then, that Dr. Goebbels called it "a dagger pointed at the heart of Germany."

In 1935, the pro-Hitler Sudeten-German party got two-thirds of all German votes in Czechoslovakia's general election (forty-four of three hundred seats in the legislature), largely because its leader, Konrad Henlein, had received both his orders and massive secret subsidies from the Nazis in neighboring Germany. In May of 1938, Hitler told his generals. "It is my unalterable decision to smash Czechoslovakia by military action in the near future." The Czechs chose not to resist the invasion when it came, relying instead on their great friends, the Western powers—and this proved a tragic mistake.

On September 29, 1938, the prime ministers of Britain and France, Neville Chamberlain and Edouard Daladier, joined Hitler and Italy's Benito Mussolini in signing the infamous Munich Pact. The agreement gave Hitler the German areas of Czechoslovakia, led to further dismemberment by the Poles and Hungarians, and virtually invited German invasion. Less than six months later, on March 15, 1939, the Germans occupied Czechoslovakia through Bohemia and Moravia. The country remained under German domination until the end of the war.

The following August 23, the foreign ministers of Germany and the Soviet Union, Joachim von Ribbentrop and V.M. Molotov, signed a non-aggression treaty, a fine example of détente that provided mutual guarantees of neutrality in any future European conflicts—and the West reluctantly steeled itself for war. The treaty, of course, did not keep Hitler from invading the Soviet Union two years later, on June 22, 1941, thus ensuring that the holocaust of war would be on a scale never before imagined. Helplessly trapped between the contending superpowers, Czechoslovakia lost 300,000 citizens before the war's end.

In Hungary, the last Habsburg, Charles I, had informally surrendered the reins of government in 1918 to Count Mihály Károlyi, a conservative aristocrat with solid democratic views who became prime minister. Hungary, like many countries in Central Europe, had minority problems, and

Károlyi soon found that he was unable to cope with the demands of the Croats, Slovaks, and Romanians under his jurisdiction. In March, 1919, the Communist leader Béla Kun seized power, but his domination lasted only a few months and was succeeded by a counterrevolution. An election in January, 1920, was based on universal suffrage, but the Social Democrats boycotted the election and the Communists were excluded by law. The right-wing coalition elected in this vacuum decided to call Hungary a kingdom, not a republic. There was no agreement on who should be king—the neighboring countries made it clear they would not permit the restoration of the Habsburg dynasty—and by way of uneasy compromise Admiral Miklós von Horthy was elected regent for a nonexistent royalty. Hungary thus remained a curious kingdom without a king until World War II.

Count Stephen Bethlen, a Calvinist nobleman from Transylvania, was the real ruler of Hungary during the 1920s as prime minister; he restored economic stability and enforced a measure of legality but opposed democracy as a political system. The country was dominated by the gentry, landowners, civil servants, high-ranking officers, and a few intellectuals. Economic stability ended in the summer of 1931, when the collapse of the Creditanstalt in nearby Vienna affected Hungary's credit system and its currency. Unemployment and extremism brought to power the right-wing leader General Julius von Gömbös, a man who admired Mussolini and tried to become a Hungarian Duce or Führer. Liberal writers in Budapest's coffeehouses laughed at the general, but he succeeded in propagating a new fascist ideology among younger Hungarians. Gömbös died in 1936 during a visit to Germany, but he had prepared the country for what was to come. Thereafter Nazi groups such as the Arrow Cross party, which took its methods and money from Hitler's Germany, began to appear in Hungary. The party's program was vague and mystical, preaching anti-Semitism and land reform and trying to appeal to extremists as well as unemployed workers. In the parliamentary elections of 1939, the Hungarian Nazis won 43 of 260 seats in the parliament.

Nevertheless, there were strong remnants of liberalism in Hungary. A group of socially conscious young writers, the March Front, demanded social reforms in the villages and courageously denounced the demagogic Arrow Cross maneuvers. The liberal paper *Magyar Nemzet* criticized the Fascist and Nazi movements; Liberals and Social Democrats attacked the government; and there was talk of political liberty and national independence. Hungary's spiritual elite had not forgotten the heritage of Sándor Petöfi, their greatest poet, and Lajos Kossuth, the patriot, and when Budapest was occupied by the Germans on March 22, 1944, there were no quislings to be found in Hungary.

There was no semblance of democracy, liberalism, or social freedom in either Yugoslavia or Romania between the two world wars; in both countries monarchs established dictatorships. Yugoslavia's history was dominated by a continuous struggle between the Serbs and Croats and the peoples of Slovenia, Voivodina, Bosnia, Montenegro, and Macedonia. King Alexander, who introduced royal dictatorship by dismissing the parlia-

The domed cathedral of Esztergom, which caps a low promontory overlooking the Danube, is said to be the most beautiful church in Hungary. That nation's first king, Stephen, was crowned in Esztergom in A.D. 1000, and since that time the former capital has been the seat of Hungary's archbishop.

At Visegrad, once the country seat of Hungary's kings, long-abandoned castles stand silent sentry on the banks of the Danube. It is here, some thirty miles north of Budapest, that the great river turns almost directly south, its pent-up waters spreading out across the vast expanse of the Hungarian Plain.

ment in 1929, never bothered to examine the underlying reasons for these social and national conflicts. Alexander constantly spoke of "a new Yugoslav patriotism" that he hoped might replace regional patriotism, but he relied for backing on the Serbs, and as a result Serbian nationalists began to regard Croatia as enemy territory. The Croats, on the other hand, complained that they were treated like a colony and taxed inordinately.

There was considerable corruption and brutality displayed on both sides, but it did not prepare either Serbs or Croats for the assassination of King Alexander in Marseilles in 1934 by a Macedonian revolutionary. For a time, at least, national differences were forgotten. Alexander's will had named his cousin, Prince Paul, as regent for his son Peter. Paul, who had been educated in England, did not understand the problems of his country and preferred to devote himself to the collecting of fine art. He was unable to establish domestic peace, and although he was terrified of bolshevism he was unable to halt its spread.

No parallels are ever truly exact in the Balkans, but Romania, too, had its royal dictatorship between the wars. Although defeated in the field by Germany in World War I, the Romanians had boldly demanded that their former ally, Russia, cede the partly Romanian province of Bessarabia to them. They quickly signed a separate peace treaty with Germany and went to the Versailles peace conference as an "Allied State." This caused hilarity among the foregathered diplomats, who said that to be Romanian was a profession, not a nationality. It also caused some indignation. Georges Clemenceau, no fool, had nothing but contempt for the Romanians, but because he and many other Western leaders were desperately frightened of bolshevism, they were glad to have a revitalized Romania next to Russia as "a bulwark against bolshevik poison." For the next two decades Romanian propagandists brilliantly exploited their country's "mission as a Christian outpost in the East." The Romanians happily declared war on Russia in 1941, and some units committed terrible massacres in the Soviet Union.

During most of the 1920s Romania was ruled by Liberals who were liberal in name only. They relied on a corrupt bureaucracy, administrative centralization, and high taxation of the peasants to maintain themselves in power. In 1930 Prince Carol, the son of former King Ferdinand, appeared in Bucharest. Owing to a morganatic marriage, he had been forced to renounce the throne and had been living a playboy's life in France. Now he wanted to be king, and he obliged the ministers to accept him as King Carol II. A flamboyant would-be dictator and a great admirer of Mussolini, Carol loved power and demagogy. Romania had never been known for the high ethical standards of its administration, but under Carol corruption and brutality became worse than ever. The terrorist organization called the Iron Guard became a powerful mass movement that was openly fascist and anti-Semitic.

In the end Carol was destroyed by the very monster he had created; an Iron Guard revolt forced him to abdicate in favor of his son, Michael, in 1940. King Michael never tried to bridge the abyss between the few who ruled with brutal force and the vast majority of the ruled. The rulers naturally supported fascism because they were all afraid of bolshevism, but the Romanian soldiers who died in the ruins of Odessa and Stalingrad never understood why they had been sent there.

In January, 1939—after Munich, but nine months before Hitler launched World War II—Graham Hutton wrote in the preface to *Survey After Munich:* "The leading motif of this book is that . . . from Danubian destiny will come European destiny. It may be peace or war, welfare or ill-fare. . . . it is a common destiny which confronts all nations in Europe."

It was to be war and ill-fare, eventually confronting most of the civilized nations on earth.

7

The Red Danube

*N*ear Vienna's Danube Canal—which follows the river's primordial course while the Danube itself, diverted to the east a century ago, cuts a new channel between the old city and Floridsdorf—stands the headquarters of the company that once controlled the entire river. Among the founders of the firm, the First Imperial Privileged Danube Steamship Company, was that professional empire builder, Prince Metternich. And among the major shareholders, when the company was set up on March 13, 1829, were the emperor of Austria and the kings of Bavaria and Württemberg. The company inaugurated regular boat service along the middle Danube in 1831, eventually extending its connecting lines all the way downriver to Galati (see map, pages 6–7) and across the Black Sea to Constantinople. In its great days, under Emperor Francis Joseph, DDSG, the Donau-Dampf-schiffahrts-Gesellschaft, was the world's largest inland shipping company and carried more than two million tons of goods a year.

The peace treaty ending the Crimean War in 1856 established the European Danube Commission. Among its members were Austria, Hungary, Russia, and Turkey—the countries then controlling the navigable stretches of the river—and also faraway Prussia, England, France, and Italy. The latter nations had no business being there except the business of power politics. A major practical purpose in forming the commission was to dredge and clear the delta of the mighty river, a task that proved extremely difficult to accomplish. "The entrance to the Sulina branch (the largest of the delta's three arms) was a wide-open seaboard strewn with wrecks and hulls," the commission's chief engineer wrote as late as 1873. "Masts sticking out of the water were used as buoys and lighthouses, the only guides to where the deepest channel was found." In this region the Danube has preserved some of its majestic force; it is still the great river that it was many thousands of years ago.

The Congress of Berlin in 1878 extended the life of the Danube Commission and five years later the Treaty of London established spheres of influence and competence along the Danube. The plenipotentiaries of the Great Powers signed a voluminous document that redefined the supranational authority of the Danube Commission—a body with its own flag, uniforms, laws, and revenue—and, in the process, exacerbated the power struggle in the Balkans. The various regimes in that part of the world were always plotting against each other, and czarist Russia, although disturbed by grave internal problems, never averted its gaze from the Danube region, ever ready to move into any power vacuum that might develop along the lower river. In their wildest dreams the czars never dared to hope that Russia might one day control virtually the entire river from source to delta, yet changes were bound to occur. For one thing, Turkey was growing steadily weaker. For another, the Dual Monarchy of Austria-Hungary, united in its belief that the acquisition of new territories in the Danube region was vital to its imperial interests, was divided over who should administer them, the Austrians in Vienna or the Hungarians in Budapest. Francis Joseph, beset by problems of his own, attempted to steer clear of the wrangling.

Somehow, despite endemic internal dissensions, the Danube Commission functioned reasonably well until World War I. A flotilla of monitors —small but heavily armed Austro-Hungarian ships—was permitted to operate all along the river as a sort of international police force during this period, and they maintained the letter—although occasionally not the spirit—of the Treaty of London. At the beginning of World War I, however, the Austrian fleet set upon the other ships that plied the Danube. A pamphlet distributed to the population of Belgrade in 1914 began, "The Austrian-Serbian war started at eleven P.M. on July 28, 1914, as the four-inch naval cannons of the Austrian Danube monitors began shelling several districts of Belgrade. . . ."

This was the effective end of the Danube Commission. In 1917, Austria-Hungary and Germany, still hopeful of winning the war, drafted a new convention that restricted permission to use the river "to the riparian states." Near the Iron Gate a towrope railroad was constructed with a track about one mile long; powerful freight locomotives, operating along its rails, could slowly tug ships through the strong currents of this dangerous section of the stream. Nothing could be done, however, to improve the dangerous political currents in the delta region, which the front lines bisected.

The end of World War I made the 1917 draft convention a worthless piece of paper. The Treaty of Versailles decreed the internationalization of the Danube and its navigable tributaries from Ulm to the Black Sea, and the later treaties of St. Germain, Neuilly, and Trianon confirmed the Versailles pact. Subsequently, all rivercraft were redistributed among the riparian states—and Austria's DDSG lost a large part of its tonnage.

The Danube Commission in Galati resumed its activities in 1918, but its jurisdiction was confined to a short section of the river in the delta region. The International Commission in Bratislava, Czechoslovakia, was to control navigation between Braila, Romania, and Ulm, Germany—and a separate authority at Orsova was to regulate passage through the Iron Gate. Freedom of navigation and international status of the Danube were reiterated by Great Britain, France, and the United States, cosignatories of a new Danube convention in 1921; three years later, no less than fifteen dif-

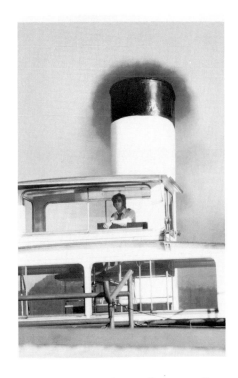

Slipping its moorings at Passau, a Danubian steamship begins its week-long voyage to the Black Sea that includes stops in all eight countries that comprise the great Danube Basin.

ferent shipping companies were operating on the river. Those located in Regensburg, Vienna, Bratislava, and Budapest promptly formed a cartel, a tentative mini-federation. Grains and ore were shipped upstream; finished products—weighing much less but costing much more—went downstream, thereby creating a permanent financial imbalance and eventually large losses for the eastern countries.

The outbreak of World War II naturally brought an end to efforts at international control of the Danube. By mid-1944, when Soviet armies were on the offensive on all fronts, Russia's leaders revived the czarist concept of power politics and moved into the power vacuum in the Balkans. Combining military force and political threats, they swiftly and brilliantly established their hegemony over the lower Danube. It all began on August 23, 1944, when King Michael of Romania had his pro-Nazi prime minister, Ion Antonescu, arrested, announced that Romania was no longer at war with the Allies, and ordered his army to stop firing at the approaching Red Army. The Germans, informed that they would be permitted to withdraw peacefully from Romania, responded by bombing Bucharest in general and the royal palace in particular. On August 25, King Michael declared war on Germany, and Romanian troops who had fought alongside the Germans for the first years of the war suddenly turned on their allies. Romania had already lost half a million men fighting for the Nazis; it would lose another 150,000 fighting against them. King Michael's move, preceded by the decision of the Big Three at the Teheran Conference not to open a front in the Balkans, handed the lower Danube to Stalin.

The Red Army marched quickly through Romania, and on September 5 reached the border of Bulgaria—whereupon that country, which had considered itself neutral, also declared war on Germany. Three days later the Red Army marched into Bulgaria, and twenty-four hours later the communist-oriented Fatherland Front seized power in Sofia. Bulgarian troops, fighting on the left flank of the Red Army, advanced to Belgrade, which was liberated from the Germans on October 20. Within less than eight weeks the Soviet Union had established hegemony over the Danube from its delta all the way to Belgrade—doing far better than Prince Eugene or any other earlier conqueror had ever been able to do. Bulgarian and Yugoslav units joined the Red Army as it swept through Croatia, Hungary, and all the way to Vienna. They stopped only when they reached the Enns Bridge, not far from Linz, and only because the Americans were on the other side.

In Hungary, meanwhile, Admiral Horthy tried to surrender to the Russians but was kidnapped by the Germans. Many Hungarian troops continued to fight on under the leadership of Ferenc Szálasi, a member of the Arrow Cross faction. By the year's end there was complete chaos and utter terror in and around Budapest. Many still remember that during the Soviet siege the Germans, joined by Hungarian fascist units, murdered and raped in the city while the Soviets and their allies did the same on the outskirts of the capital. In the final days, the Germans blew up all the Danube bridges of Budapest. Nearly 80 percent of some parts of the city were destroyed; Budapest suffered almost as much damage as Warsaw. But the

As the sun rises over its bow, the steamship Volga *slides serenely under the Iron Curtain at Bratislava. From here on the ship will navigate waters that are directly or indirectly controlled by that most extensive of all Danube empires, the Russian. Ironically, the U.S.S.R. actually controls only four miles of the river's delta—but its influence extends 1,100 miles upriver.*

Hungarian capital was liberated by the Russian army on February 13, 1945.

Farther to the northwest, the Red Army and the American army both raced toward Prague, the heart of Europe. The Germans still controlled the Czech capital in the first days of May, when the people of Prague rose against their conquerors. Earlier that year it had been agreed at the Yalta Conference that American troops would not advance beyond a line in western Bohemia running from Pilsen to Budejovice. General Eisenhower realized the immense strategic position of Prague, and knowing that Patton's Third Army had advanced rapidly toward the city while the Red Army was held back by some German suicide units in Moravia, Eisenhower suggested in an urgent, personal message to General Antonov, the chief of the Soviet general staff, that Patton's forces relieve Prague and stop Czechs and Germans from killing one another there. General Antonov angrily turned down the suggestion; Prague, he insisted, would be liberated by the Soviets. Obedient to Antonov's wishes, the Americans stayed in Pilsen—and their decision to allow the Red Army to liberate Prague proved as fateful as the one King Michael had made earlier in Bucharest. Michael had effectively handed over the Balkans to Stalin; the West's failure to take Prague ensured that Central Europe would also be dominated by the Soviets. Thus by the war's end, Soviet control of the Danube region was complete.

Military historians will long argue whether the Western Allies should have undertaken a Balkan invasion during the final phase of World War II, to prevent King Michael from surrendering to the Red Army and, possibly, to save the Danube region from Soviet domination. The fact remains that they did not launch such an invasion, and consequently, during the following three years various "people's republics" were set up under Soviet hegemony in the countries of central and southeastern Europe. At the time, apologists for the new regimes sought to persuade the rest of the world that these republics were similar in conception to Western democracies, only a little more to the left. In truth, of course, the two kinds of democracy had little in common—a fact that was later officially confirmed by the Communists themselves.

During the immediate postwar period, the official line in the countries of the Danube region was that the Red Army had defeated the Germans—which was the truth but not the whole truth, since the Western Allies had certainly contributed to the defeat by helping to arm the Russian army and by defeating Hitler in the west. In these countries, Soviet domination generally proceeded by several stages, though the chain of events was not always identical. In all countries people were elated that the terrible war was over and that the hated Germans had disappeared; in some countries optimists hoped for good relations with the East and the West, and coalition governments were set up. But even at this early stage the local Communists were close to the centers of power: they had, as often as not, infiltrated the police, the general staff of the army, and the ministry of the interior. In some countries, this first stage of domination was also the final one.

A second stage of Soviet domination occurred in countries where noncommunist bourgeois or peasant parties were permitted to form a limited

opposition. Freedom of speech and of the press also proved limited. In Hungary, the pseudo-opposition stage ended in February, 1947, when Béla Kovács of the Smallholders party was arrested by Soviet soldiers and simply disappeared. In 1947 opposition leaders were also arrested in Bulgaria, where a show trial of agrarian leader Nikola Petkov was conducted while "spontaneous demonstrations" all over the country demanded the death sentence for the accused. To no one's surprise, Petkov was executed. During the third and final stage of domination, the Soviets established outright communist regimes with a united workers' party or a communist front that former Socialists were compelled to join.

In retrospect at least, the most fortunate of the Danube countries occupied by the Soviets after World War II was Austria. The Moscow Declaration of 1943, signed by Britain, the United States, and the Soviet Union, promised the restoration of a free, independent, and democratic Austria, and the four-power declaration of July 4, 1945, declared Austria's restoration to its 1937 frontiers. (Ever since, the Austrians have claimed that their country was liberated while Germany was occupied. This does not endear the Austrians to the Germans, who remember the Austrians' enthusiasm for *Anschluss* and point out that Hitler was an Austrian.) Initially, the country was divided into four occupation zones. Lower Austria, Burgenland, and the part of Upper Austria on the left bank of the Danube went to Russia. Upper Austria on the right bank of the Danube and the province of Salzburg became the American Zone. Two western provinces, Vorarlberg and the Tyrol, were given to the French; two southern ones, Styria and Carinthia, to the British.

Vienna, located inside the Russian Zone, was governed by a special four-power statute and was connected with the West by two official corridors. Americans and French had to travel to and from Vienna via the Enns River bridge, the British via Semmering and Wiener Neustadt. There was no Allied airport in the city; both the American airport at Tulln and the Anglo-French airport of Schwechat were inside the Soviet Zone—and thus there could have been no Allied airlift to Vienna, as there was to Berlin, had one been necessary.

The city of Vienna, like the country itself, was divided into four sectors of occupation. The historical Inner City became the so-called International Sector, administered by the four powers in monthly rotation. (The Soviet-occupied Grand Hotel was one block from the American-occupied Hotel Bristol and two blocks from the British-occupied Hotel Sacher.) Until 1948 American officers were, from time to time, invited to the Soviet officers' mess at the Grand Hotel to feast on caviar and vodka, and there were evenings when the Americans reciprocated. But after the beginning of the Cold War there was no such social intercourse and the Russians rarely left

Originally two cities—Buda, on the far bank of the Danube and Pest, on the near—the twin capitals of Hungary are linked today by a series of magnificent suspension bridges.

No city in the Danube Basin has conducted such a sustained love affair with the river as has Budapest. The Hungarian capital's foremost public buildings—including the royal castle, Coronation Church, and Parliament (above)—sit at the river's edge, and the citizens of Budapest depend upon the Danube for supplies, recreation, even nourishment (right). The surrounding hills provide a pleasant spot (left) from which to view the liberation statue (right, above) erected by the Soviets after World War II.

The long history of the Danube Basin, one of the oldest continually inhabited regions on earth, has been marked by sporadic outbursts of violence—a pattern that holds true to this day. Soviet domination of Eastern Europe, achieved with little difficulty in the political vacuum that followed World War II, has been repeatedly challenged ever since. The brutally suppressed Hungarian Revolution of 1956 is the most famous and compelling of these foredoomed outpourings of nationalistic fervor.

their club—which happened to be in Emperor Francis Joseph's old palace.

The Russian mania for spy-thriller secrecy turned the baroque palaces of Vienna's fourth district, once the city's aristocratic section, into a gloomy labyrinth of ruins and mysterious courtyards. There they installed their M.V.D. interrogation centers and prisons. (This was no secret, and Americans were unofficially cautioned not to drive in the fourth district after darkness.) The more courageous Viennese papers reported that numerous Austrians were being held in these prisons, but the exact number of arrests and kidnappings that the Russians were responsible for will never be known.

In Western intelligence circles it was often suggested that the probable reason for the Soviets' reluctance to make any overt military moves against Vienna was its value as an espionage center. It was the first stop for Iron Curtain travelers headed to the West, and agents from the people's democracies—joined, at one time or another, by the intelligence agencies of at least twenty-five nations—were known to be operating in Vienna. Each of the four occupying powers had its own network, the Russians reportedly employing more than a thousand agents. In addition, the Austrian state police and each of Austria's three political parties—the People's party, the Socialists, and the Communists—collected data on Viennese citizens, leading one American intelligence officer to estimate that more than fifteen hundred Austrians had full-time jobs as spies in Vienna.

The Soviets, who directly or indirectly controlled more than three hundred Austrian enterprises, used the profits from these operations—profits on which they refused to pay taxes—to finance the Austrian Communist party. Yet even with all this help the party never got more than 4 percent of the vote. The first provisional government in postwar Vienna, established under Russian supervision by Karl Renner, a respected Socialist who later became the first president of the Second Republic, contained a number of Communists. The Western powers, which delayed recognition of Renner's regime until after the first free, democratic elections were held in November, 1945, were naturally delighted when the People's party won eighty-five seats, the Socialists seventy-six, and the Communists only four. Austria's peasants, traditionally Catholic and conservative, had united with Socialist workers to rebuff the Soviets, whom the majority of the people of Austria hated and some even dared oppose. Realizing his country's unpopularity, the Soviet high commissioner established his headquarters not in volatile Vienna but in the once elegant spa town of Baden, where he lived in a villa formerly occupied by Crown Prince Rudolf.

In the early postwar years, few people in Austria had any hope that the Soviets would ever sign the much-deferred Austrian peace treaty. But on May 15, 1955, the Viennese greeted with surprise and delight the Russians' sudden decision to sign the Austrian State Treaty in Prince Eugene's beautiful Belvedere Palace. To this day, the Austrians do not really know why the Russians gave up Austria; it was enough that they did so. The Austrians waited until the last Soviet soldier had left their country, then celebrated by opening their rebuilt State Opera with Beethoven's *Fidelio*, a song of love and freedom.

In contrast, Czechoslovakia could not escape Sovietization. Even before the end of the war, it was proclaimed that the restored republic would be a coalition of independent parties, all of which existed before the German invasion. This created the temporary illusion that Masaryk's democracy would be revived, but a closer look revealed that the Communists already controlled the police through the ministry of interior; the army through General Ludvik Svoboda, today his country's president; public opinion through the ministry of information; and soon the ministry of agriculture.

The Red Army left Czechoslovakia in late 1945 and the first free, secret parliamentary elections were held in May, 1946. The Communist party won 38 percent of the vote; the National Socialists garnered only 18 percent; and other parties fared even less well. The real turning point came on July 7, 1947, when Czechoslovakia accepted an official invitation to a preliminary Marshall Plan conference in Paris. The following day, Prime Minister Klement Gottwald and Jan Masaryk, the son of the country's founder and first president, received an ultimatum from Stalin. They would have to decide at once whether they considered "the Pact of Friendship between our countries" valid or preferred to go to Paris. Two days later it was announced that the Czechs had reluctantly agreed to reject the invitation.

Czechoslovakia's decision proved fateful not only for the country but for all countries in Eastern Europe. Everywhere popular front governments collapsed, and all the countries of the Danube Basin were obliged to join the communist organization known as Cominform. Gottwald then began a crude but effective purge of the Czech government. President Eduard Benes eventually found himself cut off from his advisers, his ministers, and from the army. General Svoboda ordered the troops to remain neutral; the Soviet ambassador threatened a Red Army invasion; and on February 25, 1948, Benes capitulated and asked Gottwald to form a new government. The only important noncommunist member of this regime was Jan Masaryk, who was named foreign minister because he enjoyed such great prestige in the West. Two weeks later, on March 10, Masaryk jumped—or, more probably, was pushed—out of the window of the Foreign Office. The process of Stalinization was complete.

Czechoslovakia experienced a brief interlude of freedom during the Prague Spring of 1968 when Alexander Dubcek replaced Antonin Novotny, an old-line Stalinist, as first secretary of the Communist party. The flurry of independence ended in August when the Soviets and their Warsaw Pact allies invaded Czechoslovakia. Dubcek was eventually expelled from the party and is today officially a nonperson with an unimportant job in his native city of Bratislava on the Danube.

The new Yugoslavia emerged on October 20, 1944, after liberation by the Red Army. It consisted of twenty-one million people—in six federated republics and two autonomous provinces—speaking half a dozen different languages, practicing three different religions, and using two different alphabets. There were considerable minorities of Albanians, Hungarians, Turks, Slovaks, Gypsies, Bulgarians, and Romanians—in short, worse than Habsburg Austria. Yet the improbable new nation was united by the pres-

"Let us request the departure of people who misused their power, damaged public property, behaved dishonestly or cruelly," the manifesto began. It called not for independence but merely for communism "with a new face"—and it launched the bittersweet Prague Spring of 1968. Czechs spoke of renaissance, of the Prague of Masaryk, Capek, Rilke, and Kafka, but the Kremlin saw only the Prague of Jan Hus. And so the tanks rolled again, and yet another spontaneous national uprising was crushed.

tige and the personality of Marshal Tito, a former Croat peasant and authentic national hero revered by his countrymen. Tito at first led the republic along Socialist and Soviet lines, but after being expelled from the Cominform in 1948 for failing to show proper reverence toward the Soviet Union, Yugoslavia became increasingly independent.

Since the days of the czars, the Russians have known that to gain control of the Danube region they would have to offer a substitute for the strong and confusing currents of nationalism in the Balkans. Pan-Slavism—the peaceful unification of all Slavs—was soon ruled out as a possible substitute, since it would not appeal to the Hungarians and Romanians but make them feel surrounded by Russians, Bulgarians, Poles, Czechs, Slovaks, and Yugoslavs. On the other hand, communism—forceful unification under Moscow's leadership—created a strong supranationalist power—and with the single exception of Yugoslavia the Danube countries were controlled by Stalin's terror and "protected" by Red Army divisions after 1948.

The legend of Soviet Army protection was first exposed for what it really was in East Berlin on June 17, 1953. On that day a mass demonstration for lower work norms welled into open rebellion that was brutally put down by Soviet T-34 tanks. Then, on October 23, 1956, the revolt of the Hungarians against their Soviet-dominated regime began in Budapest near the left bank of the Danube at the monument of Sándor Petöfi, the great poet who had inspired the country's 1848 revolution. There 200,000 people, carrying red, white, and green Hungarian flags, faced the students of the Marx-Lenin Institute, the elite of Hungary's communist youth, who were carrying red flags. "For a crucial long moment," an eyewitness remembers, "the two groups stood in silence. Suddenly the red flags were lowered and disappeared, and people stepped on them. The two groups merged. . . . We Hungarians were no longer divided." On the third day the cry went up, "Get the Russians out!"

That cry was heard by Russians as well as Hungarians, and the former responded with equal fervor and greater force: the revolution—which was not started by workers or soldiers, the classic revolutionaries, but by poets and professors, writers and intellectuals—was brutally put down by Soviet tanks. When it was all over in early November, Budapest looked as if it had been through a major battle. The Freedom Fighters, those not dead or wounded, had escaped to Austria—and more than 200,000 Hungarians eventually followed them.

But life went on afterward, and the people of Budapest were supported by a universally held love for their city. No other nation along the Danube has such strong feelings about its capital and the river that winds through its heart. All the city's great buildings, whether in Buda on the left bank, or in Pest on the right, face the river—the neo-Gothic Houses of Parliament, the Coronation Church, the Royal Palace, the old palaces on the hills above Buda. Many of the structures on the banks of the river have recently been given new, gaily colored façades, and buildings along the embankment are generally in better repair than those set farther back.

The people of Budapest take special pride in their bridges; all of them were destroyed by the Germans in 1945 as they escaped from Pest to Buda, where they were at last surrounded by the Red Army. The destruction of the bridges was a terrible blow to civic pride, but in ten years all were rebuilt. In Vienna, the first major postwar rebuilding project was the State Opera; in Budapest it was the Liberty Cantilever Bridge.

The oldest of Budapest's Danube bridges is the Széchényi Suspension Bridge, built by the English engineer William Tierney Clark and opened in 1849. The last to be restored was the Empress Elizabeth Bridge, a single span of 290 meters that was considered a technical wonder when it was opened in 1903. When the people of Budapest are not promenading on their beloved bridges they are strolling on the Korzó, the city's famous riverside walkway, or relaxing on Margaret Island in the middle of the Danube. That island, used two thousand years ago as a playground by the Romans, is now a magnificent park and recreation area replete with hot springs, boathouses, hotel, open-air cinemas, and an amphitheater.

Today, first nights at the Budapest Opera are almost as elegant as first nights in Milan, London, Vienna, or New York. The city's best hotels compare favorably with those in the West, and its nightclubs are called by experts "the best on the Continent." No one is able to explain satisfactorily how so many people can afford to live as they do, but Hungarians are virtuoso *débrouillards* and they have much experience in adapting to strong regimes. Significantly, fully one third of those who fled after the revolution have returned, and János Kádár, once the hated puppet of the Soviets, now enjoys the affection of a large part of the population.

In 1948, shortly before Marshal Tito was ejected from the Cominform, the Soviet Union and its Danube Basin satellites met in Belgrade. This

For more than three hundred miles of its lower course the Danube forms the common border between Romania and its neighbor to the south, Bulgaria. The river flows almost due east at this point —and it seems to flow backward into time. The peasants who live along the silt-laden, slow-moving lower Danube appear born of another age.

Below Belgrade the gray waters of the Danube are funneled through a keyhole in the Carpathians known as the Iron Gate. Suddenly falling more than one hundred feet, the roiling river roars through the Kazan Defile (opposite) and empties onto the broad Wallachian Plain below. In recent years this great cataract has been partially tamed by the immense Djerdap High Dam (above), a hydroelectric plant that is jointly administered by Romania and Bulgaria.

conference of the Eastern bloc declared the 1921 Danube convention null and void and established a new, Soviet-dominated Danube Commission. The United States, Great Britain, and France refused to accept the decisions of the Belgrade conference, but the Soviet Union—which, ironically, controls only four kilometers of the Danube's total length—hardly cared.

Since 1948 the other riparian states have made the best of their difficult political situation. In 1953, for example, Austria and Hungary agreed on mutual navigational facilities, and similar agreements were later signed between other states. Whether the Danubian states, especially those sharing borders, will ever overcome their historical prejudices and national conflicts is something no student of Balkan politics would want to predict. Pessimists would cite the example of the Sofia-to-Bucharest rail link as a case in point. For many years the main rail line out of Sofia, Bulgaria's capital, ran north to Ruse on the Danube, an old Roman port that was used by the Austro-Hungarian Danube flotilla in World War I. From Giurgiu, on the Romanian side of the river, a second railroad continued north to Bucharest, that nation's capital. Both railroad lines ended at the banks of the river, separated by one mile of water. For decades there was talk of building a bridge to link the two lines, but that span was not actually constructed until 1954. Called Friendship Bridge, the link unfortunately reflects the architectural and technical precepts of the Stalinist era, and today both Romanians and Bulgarians agree that the bridge should have been constructed in a more simple and functional way. Moreover, friendship is a much misused word in the Balkans, still a breeding ground of intrigue. Romania, for instance, still demands the return of Bessarabia and northern Bucovina from the Soviet Union, and Hungary would like to get Transylvania back from Romania.

Three times a month between March and November, the motor ships

Volga and *Dnepr* of SDGP, the Soviet Danube Steamship Line, leave Passau, Germany, and arrive a week later at Ismail, the Soviet bridgehead in the Danube delta—having come by way of Vienna, Bratislava, Budapest, Belgrade, Ruse, and Giurgiu. The ships are popular with tourists from the West, possibly because they offer a swimming pool; Russian delicacies such as borscht, Kiev cutlets, shashlik, and caviar; side excursions through many Danubian capitals; and the splendid scenery of the valley itself.

Travelers agree that the journey along the middle Danube, from Bratislava to the Iron Gate, is the most fascinating. This is the Danube of vast plains, green meadows, and small riverside villages where people sip plum brandy and drink strong Turkish coffee, the Danube of the Huns and Avars, Slavs and Turks. After the Hungarian Plain come the flat green and brown fields of Voivodina, which Serbians, Hungarians, and Romanians once fought over. The most dramatic section of the Danube journey occurs between Yugoslavia and Romania, at the Gorge of Kazan and the Iron Gate—eight miles of cataracts that suddenly narrow the river to two-thirds of its former width. Yugoslavia and Romania have recently built a vast lock and dam system that takes the danger out of this passage, and a large power plant now utilizes the river's hidden energies.

After the excitement of the Iron Gate the journey farther downstream, between Bulgaria and Romania, is largely anticlimactic. A sense of timelessness hovers over this part of the river, which is dominated by the black hills of Bulgaria, for five hundred years home to the Turks. The Danube now becomes a definite frontier between the high cliffs of Bulgaria and the woods and plains of Romania, where the government has created enormous iron, steel, and chemical industries in Galati and Braila. The Danube is no longer a river but a system of channels, islands, lakes, and marshes. In the south is the coastal strip of Dobruja, in the north the Baragan Steppe, made famous by the Romanian poet Panait Istrati, "the Gorki of the Balkans."

The Danube delta is a wasteland filled with tow flax that grows in the inlets and is harvested from small punts. It is also a paradise for water birds and water buffalo, for wolves and wild boars. The region was once famous for the hundreds of thousands of white pelicans that nested there, but of these only two thousand pairs are believed to survive. Large sturgeon sometimes enter the mouth of the Danube to spawn, and the production of caviar has become a minor industry along the riverbanks. (Soviet scientists have found more than a hundred different kinds of fish and three hundred species of birds in the delta.) Below Ismail, the Danube's three arms—the Chilia, Sulina, and the Saint George—carry its silt-laden waters to the Black Sea—and in this final stretch it is often impossible to say where the river ends and the sea begins.

The chief lesson to be learned from the tragic history of the Danube region is that no one ever learns from history, no matter how often it repeats itself. Looking at two thousand years of successive conquest and defeat, brutal war and uneasy peace, one wonders at persistent human optimism. So many have thought that they could succeed where others had failed, but invasion, war, and terror settle nothing in the long run—they only breed more terror. Paradoxically, the only major power to truly dominate the Danube region, the Soviet Union, was never directly involved in the battles for the river. Russia lost millions of men in World War II, but not primarily in contests for domination of the lands in the Danube region.

The Habsburgs, who tried for more than seven hundred years to extend their holdings all the way from the source of the Danube to the delta, sacrificed the lives of millions but never managed to penetrate beyond the Iron Gate, where the borders of Yugoslavia, Bulgaria, and Romania meet. The Habsburgs' successors, the Nazis, were for a brief time able to expand this Danube empire to the east. In doing so they partially satisfied those who promoted the Danube as Germany's *Schicksalsfluss*. Obedient to the demands of destiny, the Third Reich sacrificed vast quantities of men and matériel to establish a Danube regime from Austria, Czechoslovakia, and Hungary all the way to Yugoslavia, Bulgaria, and Romania. After a short time, however, the Germans were driven out of these lands, which they were neither politically nor militarily prepared to rule. And now the Soviets, who allegedly pay little attention to the lessons of the past and follow Lenin's precepts for the future, control the Danube.

Politically, Soviet domination of the Danube region is absolute; economically, Soviet domination of the Danube is relative, for once again the Danube has become the major west-east commercial waterway of Europe. And as the late Dr. Leopold Figl, Austria's former chancellor, once noted, coexistence along the Danube is an economic necessity. "Austrians, Yugoslavs, Czechs, Hungarians, Bulgarians, Romanians have a vital common interest in working together," Figl wrote. "Economically, nothing on earth can keep us apart."

Since then, farsighted men have spoken of some kind of economic federation of the Danube nations. No one really believes that the Habsburg Danube empire will ever be reconstituted, but in spite of their ideological and national differences the nations of the Danube remain united by their sense of a common mission. It is now agreed on both sides of the ideological boundary line that the logical center of a Danube federation is Vienna —no longer the capital of the Danube empire but that of a small, neutral nation, an economic and cultural bridge between East and West. Two thousand years of history cannot be swept away by thirty years of Marxist doctrine, and the Austrians have longer and more extensive experience in the Danube Basin than any of the other riparian states.

The form of a future Danube federation remains vague. Ideally, it would be an alliance of free nations operating under a mutually satisfactory Danube charter. This all sounds rather utopian and unrealistic so long as Red Army forces remain encamped along the banks of the Danube. But legionnaires don't stay forever—not the Roman, nor the Habsburg, nor Hitler's legions—and long after the Red legions have disappeared the steady flow of the majestic river will continue, with a timeless rhythm and inexorable force. If the Danube could once fulfill the dream of a supranational coexistence, based on common sense and common need, it might truly become the stream of a new and better European destiny.

So vast and amorphous is the Danube Delta (left) that it is almost impossible to judge where the river ends and the sea begins. Here fresh water mingles with brine, here East fuses with West, and here the patterns of history—those that have, from time to time, altered the political color of the multihued Danube—give way to patterns of nature.

The Danube in Literature

The world's most famous waltz—and, since the turn of the century, the unofficial anthem of the Danube—is Johann Strauss's "The Blue Danube," conceived in 1867 as a choral and not an instrumental work. Inspired by the obscure poet Karl Isador Beck, Strauss created his musical tribute to the river for the Viennese Men's Choral Association, which promptly had words set to it. These banal lyrics, penned by Viennese police clerk Joseph Weyl, bear mentioning only because they contributed to the indifference with which glittering Viennese society greeted the new waltz on opening night. It took the equally glittering society of France's Second Empire—on the occasion of that year's Paris Exposition—to recognize the magic in Strauss's melody and to rescue it from obscurity, whereupon it became the musical toast of the Continent. Still performed regularly at Austrian state functions, "The Blue Danube" has been paired since 1890 with the more felicitous lyrics of Franz Gernerth.

The Danube, perhaps more than any other river, has seen its share of catastrophes. The Thirty Years' War (1618–48) began as a local revolt in Bohemia, then evolved into a continent-wide conflict between Catholics and Protestants, one mainly fought on German soil. Before completing its savage course, the war carried vast areas of Central Europe—including the lands along the Danube—to the threshold of ruin. In 1636, England's King Charles I, hoping to hammer out a compromise agreement between Europe's feuding princes, dispatched the earl of Arundel on a peace mission to the court of Ferdinand II, Holy Roman Emperor and leader of the Catholic faction. While Arundel's party was traveling down the Danube as far as Linz, site of the emperor's palace, William Crowne, a servant to the earl, recorded in his diary the details of their journey. More connoisseur than statesman, Arundel returned to England carrying many art treasures but no peace accord.

Donau, so blau,
Durch Talund Au
Wogst ruhig du hin,
Dich grüsst unser Wein,
Dein silbernes Band
Knüpft Land an Land,
Und fröhliche Herzen
 Schlagen an deinem
  schönen Strand.
Weit vom Schwarzwald
Her eilst du hin zum Meer,
Spendest Segen alter
 wegen,
Ostwärts geht dein Lauf,
Nimmst viel Brüder auf:
Bild der Einigkeit
Für albe Zeit.
Alte Burgen seh'n
Nieder von den Höh'n,
Grüssen gerne
Dich von ferne,
Und der Berge Kranz,
Hell vom Morgenglanz,
Spiegelt sich in
Deiner Wellen Tanz.

Danube so blue,
You flow straight through
The meadows and dales
Vienna now hails
Your silvery stream
With glist'ning gleam,
For hearts that are happy
Beat on your shores and
 sweetly dream.
From the forest black
To the sea you track,
You give blessing while
 caressing,
And while flowing East,
You have never ceased
Joining shore to shore
Forever more.
Castles from on high
Watch you passing by,
Send a fleeting,
Joyful greeting,
And the mountain peak
On which sun beams streak,
Is reflected in
Your waves unique.

FRANZ GERNERTH
"The Blue Danube," 1890

On Sunday, May 22, we left Nurnburg for Regensburg, hoping to meet the Emperor there, and passed first through part of the Upper Palatinate to Newmark, in level country, where we stayed the night. Here His Excellency inspected the King of Bohemia's house adjoining the inner wall of the town; a house strengthened by bulwarks and palisadoes and possessing spacious rooms and a fine armoury.

Early next morning we set off, passing churches razed to the ground, and fearing attacks from Crabbats who lurked about the woods through which we passed, until we reached the wretched little village of Hemmaw which has been pillaged twenty-eight times in the space of two years and has been sacked twice in a single day. There is no supply of water here beyond what we collected when it rains.

After resting and having dinner here, we journeyed on to Ettershausen, a poor village where, since the bridge had been burnt down by the Swedes [the Protestant army of Gustavus Adolphus], we were compelled to cross by boats.

From hence we climbed a high hill, then after descending its reverse slope, travelled along a high ridge with the river Danube on our right hand and vines on the mountain on our left. As before, we passed through several villages that had been burnt down or destroyed, till at length we came to a garri-

soned round fort, guarding the bridge, and passing through a tower standing in the middle of it over the river Danube, arrived at His Excellency's lodging in the city of Regensburg.

At this point the river runs with a current as swift as that at London Bridge, and is split by several islands with houses built on them, but these, as also the houses built on the arches of the bridge, had been burnt down or demolished in the fighting which took place when the city was captured by the Swedes and when it was regained by the King of Hungary.

On May 25, while walking on the other side of the town, His Excellency noted the ruins of many houses and churches and, about two miles outside the city, entered a Carthusian monastery, not so damaged as the rest, which the King of Hungary used as his headquarters at the time of his recapture of Regensburg. In a cell of this same monastery the old Duke of Bavaria, father of the present Duke, spent many years of his life.

Another visit which His Excellency paid was on May 28 when he walked round a Jesuit monastery which possesses an altar dedicated to St. George.

After staying a week at Regensburg, we took four boats to travel down the Danube, through Bavaria, on our way to Lintz, passing the castle of Donaustauff on

its high summit, overlooking a village nestling on the left side of the Danube, and by Werth Castle to Straubingen, both of them on the left side.

At Straubingen we landed at about eleven o'clock at night, and after staying the night there, went on to Pogen, passing many ruins on the way. Pogen lies on the right side of the Danube at the foot of the very high mountain which is crowned by a church with a few houses round about it. . . .

The next morning, as His Excellency was embarking again, he saw, standing among the unhappy wretches begging for alms, a poor boy, with a thin and strangely-distorted face, who had neither ears nor any passage for hearing but who could, nevertheless, hear anyone who shouted loudly and could also make slight noises through his mouth and nose. With him was his sister, a pretty girl, who when anyone addressed him, used signs to help him to understand. His Excellency took the pair of them in his boat as far as our next landing place, a city called Passau, on the right of the Danube where, in addition to giving them money, he commanded that new clothes were to be made for them, after which they were to be sent home to their friends.

Passau, which is just beyond Bavaria, has a very pleasing position, with three rivers running by the city: the Danube, grey in colour, flows past one side; the white waters of the swift-running Inn, which rises in Italy, sweep past another side; while on the third side are the black waters of the Ilz, flowing out of Bohemia and, like the Inn, joining the Danube just beyond the town. . . .

The strongly-built and impregnable castle of Festingoverhouse stands on its lofty summit on the opposite bank of the Danube, commanding the town and the monasteries; while beneath the hill on which it is built, and near the confluence of the Ilz and the Danube, stands another massive fort.

The city itself is governed by Leopold, the Emperor's second son, who is its bishop. After staying here for three days, we entered Upper-Austria on June 4, passing Schaumberg Castle on the left side of the river and Effertingen, and the Wilhering monastery, on the other side.

On our arrival at Lintz, where the Emperor was staying, His Excellency was met upon landing by the Count of Harrack, Marshal of the Court, and by other courtiers. Following this friendly reception, some ten or twelve coaches arrived to convey His Excellency and our party to the lodgings provided by the Emperor for our stay here and, soon afterwards,

Count Megaw, High Steward to the Emperor, came to visit His Excellency. The next day Count Mansfelt, Captain of the Emperor's Foot Guard, followed in due course by Father Lemmerman, the Emperor's confessor, came to visit His Excellency.

On June 6, the second day of our visit, His Excellency had an audience with the Emperor and Empress, who sent their coaches to bring us to their palace, which stands on a hill. We climbed four flights of stairs with the Emperor's Guard, armed with carbines and halberds, on either side of us, then through various rooms till we came to the door of the room where the Emperor was. Out of this room came the little Count of Kezell, High Chamberlain to the Emperor, and after conducting His Excellency into the Emperor's presence, he came out of the room, closing the door after him that none might gain admittance. A little later we were allowed to enter and to kiss the Emperor's hand, after which we withdrew through other rooms and along a gallery, all guarded as before with soldiers of the Guard, till we were able to catch a glimpse of the Empress, whereupon we returned to our lodging.

WILLIAM CROWNE
Diary, 1636

On August 13, 1704, the army of Habsburg Emperor Leopold I and his allies met and defeated a much larger force of French and Bavarians representing Louis XIV and the prince of Bavaria. The great battle of Blenheim—fought at Blindheim, Germany, on the Danube—is listed in Sir William Creasy's Fifteen Decisive Battles of the World *not simply because it was a crucial engagement in the War of the Spanish Succession (1701–14) and a stunning victory for the allies, but also because it humbled conquering France and halted the eastward advance of autocratic Catholicism. Credit for the allied triumph was shared equally by an Austrian, Prince Eugene of Savoy, and an Englishman, the first duke of Marlborough. To commemorate Marlborough's victory on the Danube, a grateful England presented him with Blenheim Palace, a monumental mansion designed by John Vanbrugh. Winston Churchill, a direct descendant of Marlborough who was born at Blenheim Palace, paid several visits to the famous battlefield before preparing a massive, six-volume biography of his illustrious ancestor.*

Marlborough had spent some of the night in prayer. He received the sacrament from Dr Hare. "The religion he had learned as a boy" fortified his resolution and sealed his calm. While the advance guards were moving into the night he visited Prince Eugene, whom he found writing letters. They mounted their horses. It is said by several authorities that on being in the saddle he declared, "This day I conquer or die." Nothing was more unlike him. Months before in England he had used such words to Wratislaw, and assuredly they did not go beyond the truth. But, arrived at the point of action, it is more probable that he made some considerate inquiry about his horse's forage or his man's rations.

The army filed off at three o'clock in eight columns, preceded by 40 squadrons, along tracks which had been carefully marked and prepared, through darkness intensified by the gathering mists of dawn. As day broke they crossed the watercourse by Tapfheim, and here the advance guards were merged in their respective columns. Here also a ninth column was formed close to the [Danube]. It comprised all the troops of the outpost line, and included the two English brigades of Rowe and Ferguson, in all 20 battalions and 15 squadrons. Of this powerful body Lord Cuts took

command. The artillery and the pontoons marched by the main road with the Duke's six-horse coach at their tail. The whole force numbered 66 battalions, 160 squadrons, and 66 guns, or about fifty-six thousand men. Daylight came, but at first the sun only drew more vapours from the marshes and shrouded densely the crawling masses. Thus the heads of the columns arrived in line with Schwenningen village, scarcely two miles from the enemy's camp, about six.

Here Marlborough and Eugene remained together for some time in company with the Prussian Major-General Natzmer, who had fought at Höchstädt in the previous year. The plan of the two commanders was that Eugene should attack and hold the enemy's left wing while Marlborough overwhelmed his right. If Marlborough succeeded, he carried forward Eugene's battle with him. The more decisively Eugene could attack, the greater the chances of Marlborough's success. If both allied wings were defeated, retreat would be difficult, especially for Eugene, most of whose troops could only have fallen back into trackless wooded heights. On the other hand, the advance of Marlborough along the Danube and towards Höchstädt would not only conquer the enemy in his own front, but would threaten the retreat of the whole of the French opposite Eugene.

The mists began to thin as the sun rose higher, and the enemy outposts became aware of large numbers of men gathering along their front. They sent back speedy warnings, and at the same time the mists dispersing revealed from the French camp large forces covering the whole space from the Danube to the hills. Even now the Marshals and the Elector held to their prepossession that the confederate army was retiring under a bold display through the shallow valley which led back to Nördlingen. Tallard had finished a letter to the King, but before dispatching it he added the following postscript:

This morning before daybreak the enemy beat the *général* at 2 o'clock and at three the *assemblée*. They are now drawn up at the head of their camp, and it looks as if they will march this day. Rumour in the countryside expects them at Nördlingen. If that be true, they will leave us between the Danube and themselves and in consequence they will have difficulty in sustaining the posts and depots which they have taken in Bavaria. . . .

The French position had been selected for its military advantages. Its flanks rested securely on the Danube and the wooded hills. Its four-mile front was shielded by the rivulets of the Nebel. In those days, when populations were small and only the best soil cultivated, drainage was rare; and a strip of soft or marshy ground, in places a treacherous quag, profuse in rushes and marigold, laced by streamlets from four to twelve feet broad, carried the springs and rainfall from a wide bay of hills to the river. A spell of dry weather had reduced this obstacle, still however serious to the soldiers of 1704. Along it were three considerable villages. On the French right, a furlong of water-meadows from the Danube, stood Blenheim (locally Blindheim), about three hundred houses, many of stone, with the usual South German gardens and enclosures, clustered round a solid church and stone-walled graveyard. Two miles or more away in the centre rose the roofs and church-tower of Oberglau, and a mile and a half beyond, nestling under the hills, the spire of Lutzingen. Here were three strong points on which to hang the front. From the marshes of the Nebel the ground rose almost imperceptibly but steadily in about a mile to a grassy upland, upon which the four or five thousand French and Bavarian tents were spread in well-drawn rows. On the allies' side the slopes were slightly more pronounced; and here the villages of Weilheim and Unterglau with several smaller hamlets had served as the French outpost line. These had already been set on fire by the retiring pickets and were burning briskly. . . .

The whole front from the Danube to the hills was roaring with fire and conflict. "From one end of the armies to the other every one was at grips and all fighting at once—a feature very rare in battles." Marlborough, who had lately been watching the battle from the rising ground behind Unterglau, attended by his retinue, now came quickly forward, passed the burning villages, crossed the Nebel by a causeway, and took personal control at the danger-point. He led forward three Hanoverian battalions from Holstein-Beck's reserve. He made Colonel Blood bring a battery of cannon across the streamlet. With these he threw the Irish back some distance towards Oberglau. In this breathing-space the rest of Holstein-Beck's command began to form a line on the firm ground. This was the moment for Marsin's cavalry beyond Oberglau to renew their charges, and strenuous efforts were made to gather a strong force and set it in motion. . . .

A lull now descended upon the battlefield. The firing had lasted more than six hours. . . .

The last scene in the drama of Blenheim lay around the village which finally gave its name to the battle. The garrison comprised the best infantry of France and its proudest regiments. They had repulsed every attack with heavy slaughter and so far with no great loss to themselves. But many had seen—and it needed no military knowledge to understand—what had happened on the plain and what its consequences to them would be. Their army was routed, and they were cut off. The Marquis de Clérambault, whose nervousness or folly had crowded Tallard's reserves into the village, saw himself the cause of the disaster which had befallen the army and was now to overtake himself and all those for whom he was responsible. His brain reeled. He sought in flight a still more fearful safety. Without a word to his subordinates or giving anyone a chance to assume the command, he rode to the river, attended only by his groom. The man tried the passage and escaped: his master followed, "apparently," says Saint-Simon cruelly, "intending thereafter to live as a hermit." But the swirl of the Danube mercifully extinguished a life for which there was no room on earth. More charitable tales have been told of his conduct. He had gone to examine the river-bank —a cannon-ball had startled his horse, and he had fallen into the river; or again that he sought in its wave the death he found. . . .

The grief and fury of these . . . [French] troops have often been described. The regiment of Navarre burned its standards, and many officers refused to sign the convention; but this could hardly avail them much. Before nine o'clock the surrender was complete. It was not till then that Marlborough's orders arrived. The Duke, concerned at the very great numbers he now knew to be in the place, would run no risks. All the troops were to lie on their arms, and by morning he would bring the entire army. But the work had already been completed by his competent lieutenants. "Without vanity," wrote Orkney, "I think we did our parts." And so had they all.

WINSTON CHURCHILL
Marlborough: His Life and Times, 1934

Most English tourists of the eighteenth and nine-teenth centuries sought out the cultured comforts of accessible countries like France and Italy, forsaking the long—and often hazardous—side excursion that led through Germany and down the Danube to Vienna. Not so Dr. Charles Burney, father of the novelist Fanny Burney and author of the definitive History of Music. *Gathering material for his book and determined to reach the musical shrines of Vienna, Burney traveled extensively through Europe in 1770 and 1772, even gliding down the Danube on a log raft. The notes of his trip, published separately as* Dr. Charles Burney's Continental Travels, *explore many of the irritating inconveniences that unseasoned voyagers could expect to find on the upper reaches of the river.*

The next morning was clear, but cold. The passengers landed at Landau about ten; at one we entered the Danube, which did not appear so vast a river here as I expected. However, it grew larger as we descended: we stopped at two o'clock at a miserable village, with a fine convent in it, however. Here the wind became so violent, that I thought every minute it would have carried away both my cabin and myself; at three, it was determined to stay here all night, as it was not safe to stir during this wind; but as this seems, and is called, *Le Pays des vents*, it was an exercise for patience to be stopped at a place, where I had nothing to do. My provisions grew short and stale, and there were none of any kind to be had here! . . .

When I agreed to live night and day, for a week, upon the water, I forgot to bargain for warm weather; and now it was so cold, that I could scarcely hold the pen, though but the 27th of August! I have often observed, that when the body is cold, the mind is chilled likewise; and this was now so much the case with myself, that I had neither spirits nor ideas for working at my musical journal.

At eight o'clock we stopped at Vilshofen, a sweet situation. Here is a wooden bridge, of sixteen arches, over the Danube. The hills on the opposite side of the town are covered with wood, and exceedingly beautiful. The fog was dissipated, and the sun now shone on them in great glory. There is a gentle visit here from the custom-house officers; the seals were cut off my trunk, being the last town in Bavaria. They threatened hard as to the severe examination I was to undergo

upon entering Austria; however, I had little to lose, except time; and that was now too precious to be patiently parted with to these inquisitorial robbers.

At half an hour past nine we set off for Passau, in very fine weather, which revived my spirits, and enabled me to hold my pen. The Danube abounds in rocks, some above water, and some below, which occasion a great noise by the rapidity of the current, running over, or against them.

We met this morning a gang of boats, laden with salt, from Salzburg and Passau, dragged up the river by more than forty horses, a man on each, which expense is so great, as to enhance the price of that commodity above four hundred per cent. We did not seem to move so fast now as upon the Isar, which had frequent cascades. . . .

Thus far the Danube runs between two high mountains, and sometimes it is so compressed and shut up, as to be narrower than the Thames at Mortlake. The descent is often so considerable, that the water cannot be seen at the distance of a quarter of a mile, and sometimes the noise against rocks is as violent, and as loud as a cataract. . . .

I had now filled up the chinks of my cabin with splinters, and with hay; got a new button to the door, reconciled myself to my filthy blanket, and made a pair of snuffers out of a chip of deal; but alas! the essential failed: this was all external, and I wanted internal comfort! the last bit of my cold meat was fly-blown, to such a degree, that, ravenous as I was, I threw it into the Danube; bread too, that staff was broken! and nothing but *Pumpernickel* was to be had here; which is so black and sour, as to disgust two senses at a time. . . .

This river continues running through the same woody, wild, and romantic country; which, to pass through, is pleasant and entertaining, to a stranger, but produces nothing, except firing, to the poor inhabitants. For fifty miles not a corn field or pasture is to be seen. Sheep, oxen, calves, and pigs, are all utter strangers in this land. I asked what was behind these mountains, and was answered, huge forests. At Ashach the country opens a little.

What an aggregate of waters is here! river after river, comes tumbling into the Danube, and yet it grows rather more deep than wide, by these accessions; but many small rivers detach themselves from it, and islands are frequently formed in the middle and sides of this world of waters: before we arrived at Linz, however, a flat fenny country appeared, with high mountains, covered with trees, at a distance.

The approach to this town (Linz), by water, is very beautiful. There is a road on each side the Danube, at the foot of high mountains and rocks, covered with trees, by which the river is again bounded. The castle is seen at a distance, and houses and convents, upon the summit of some of the highest hills, have a fine appearance. There is a bridge over the Danube of twenty very wide arches. The town is built on the summit and sides of high hills, and in situation much resembles Passau. The churches were shut up, as it was twelve o'clock when we arrived; however, I obtained permission to enter the collegiate church, where I found a large organ.

There is such an appearance of piety here, as I never saw before in the most bigoted Catholic countries. All along the Danube, near any town, there are little chapels erected, at only twenty or thirty yards distance from each other, sometimes on the sides of these mountains, and in places too narrow for a foot-path; and I saw not a house in Linz that had not a Virgin or a saint, painted or carved, upon it. . . .

At Nussdorf, a village within three miles of Vienna, with nothing in it but a church and a custom-house, I was quite out of patience, at being told, that the float could not, as it was Sunday, on any account, enter Vienna. It was now but five o'clock, and the seventh day of my being immured in a sty, where, indeed I might have grown fat if I had had anything to eat; but that not being the case, hunger as well as loss of time, made me very impatient to be released; and after an hour lost in trying to procure a chaise, I at last got a miserable boat to carry me and my servant to Vienna.

This voyage added but little to my knowledge of German music, but a great deal to that of the people, and country through which I passed: indeed I had an opportunity of landing at every considerable town in the passage, where I visited the churches, though I had not time to make acquaintance with musical people, or to collect historical materials; but as to *national music*, perhaps the rude songs which I heard sung by the boors and watermen, gave me a more genuine idea of it, than is to be acquired from the corrupted, motley, and Italianized melody, to be heard in the capitals of this extensive country.

The approach to Vienna from the river, is not very unlike that of Venice, though there is much less water, for the Danube divides itself into three streams, about a mile and a half above the town; forty or fifty towers and spires may be seen from the water.

The custom-house did not disappoint my expectation of its being remarkably troublesome, particularly, in the article of *books*; all are stopped there, and read more scrupulously than at the inquisition of Bologna, in Italy; and mine, which, except music, were merely geographical and descriptive, were detained near a fortnight before I could recover them; and his excellency Lord Viscount Stormont, his majesty's ambassador at this court, afterwards told me, that this was the only thing in which it was not in his power to assist me. On entering the town, I was informed, that if a single book had been found in my . . . travelling satchel, its whole contents would have been forfeited.

DR. CHARLES BURNEY

Dr. Charles Burney's Continental Travels, 1773

When English novelist and travel writer Frances Trollope boated down the Danube to Vienna more than fifty years after Dr. Burney, the river had grown scarcely more hospitable to foreign guests. Travel was crude, accommodations primitive, and the river current treacherous in places. Yet the mother of author Anthony Trollope still found breath between complaints to wax rhapsodical on the beauty of Austria's castle-studded Wachau Valley—and especially on Castle Dürnstein, situated high on a bluff overlooking the river. Dürnstein had inflamed English imaginations since the days when Richard the Lion-Hearted, returning home from the Crusades, was imprisoned in the fortress by a vindictive noble—only to be rescued by his loyal servant Blondel, or so legend had it. The fact or fiction of the romance mattered little to Trollope, caught up as she was in the sheer natural splendor of the river setting.

The moment the boat had turned the point which hid it from us, I knew that the object which presented itself loftily alone on the hill that faced us, was Durenstein. Its high and isolated position is of itself enough to give a strong impression of its unapproachable solitude; but, as we came near enough to examine the nature of the country in which it is placed, a sensation of pity, and almost of horror, seemed common to us all, and we felt as truly that Richard was our king, as if he had reigned but yesterday.

Were I to tell you that this frightful fortress was placed on the pinnacle of a high and barren rock, I should tell you true, and yet be far from giving you a just idea of its position. It stands, indeed, upon a bleak bare rock, and it stands alone, for a precipice apparently yawns round every side of it; but this is not the feature which gives the greatest horror to the fortress of Durenstein. It is not the one barren crag on which it rears its now crumbling terrors, but the dark world of other crags that surround it, which makes this spot one of the most awful that nature ever formed. The mountain is bristled with these dark masses of all heights and amplitudes, and in forms so strangely grotesque, that it is difficult to believe they have received them from the ordinary accidents of natural formation.

Strongly were we tempted to order the captain to put us on shore at the foot of these strange rocks; but, on consulting one or two of our fellow-passengers, we found that it would be much less inconvenient to visit this singular spot from Vienna, from which it was distant forty English miles, than to quit the boat, leaving all our baggage behind us, in the hasty manner proposed. So we yielded to reason, and rowed on;—but deeply did I vow, as we stood gazing till the grim ruin was hid from our sight, that I would not leave Austria till I had stood within the walls that had held Richard [the Lion-Hearted] prisoner. . . .

I am now writing to you from a spot whence, I truly believe, no English letter was ever written before; for my great predecessor in the occupation of this rock, though most decidedly my countryman, had not much opportunity of indulging in the luxury of epistolary correspondence.

I told you, a week or two ago, when passing on the Danube under the shadow of these terrific rocks, that I was determined to return, without being under the control of either boatman or coachman, to wander at will in the dry and desolate wilderness, and find my way about the fragment of that lonely fortress, in which our first Richard was held captive.

And, true to my vow, here I am; and, scattered up and down the rocks, in most happy indulgence of their various whims, my whole party are here too, with the intention of passing one day of freedom where the poor king passed so many in captivity.

How like a chained eagle must the royal soldier

have felt while pinioned on this frightful pinnacle! I think the spot was chosen in the hope that the unequalled desolation of the scene might appal the lion's heart, and slowly kill his royal spirit, even while his imprisoned body was suffered to live.

But as I have already performed some astonishing feats of climbing, and am now enjoying myself under the cool but arid shadow of a mass of rock, with my note-book and my pen and ink, expressly for the purpose of making you a sharer in my expedition, I must begin, like all other faithful historians, at the beginning.

We left Vienna at five o'clock yesterday morning, and had a woefully tedious day's journey to Krems, where we slept last night. We breakfasted at Stockerau, and saw there twenty-eight carriages belonging to the Emperor, on their return from Prague: then passed over a country not particularly interesting, excepting that at one place we got a fine view of the Danube, and at another had the satisfaction of knowing that we were on the plain where the famous battle of Wagram was fought; and after a villainously bad dinner reached the little town of Krems too late to walk down to the river, which is at no great distance, or to look about us in what appeared to be an interesting old town. . . .

The road from Krems to Durenstein runs along the edge of the Danube, which is at this point as beautiful as any river can be, when the scene through which it passes is made up of gloom and desolation. The gasthaus at which we put up the carriage, and took our breakfast, is the remnant of an old convent, the windows of which almost hang over the river; and if the taste of the poor recluses who formerly looked from them was of the melancholy-sublime class, they must have drawn much consolation from the position.

At many points of the little town, which is now only the habitation of a few poor Vignerons, traces of its former strength are visible. The escape of Maximilian the First from his rock near Innspruck is recorded as a miracle; but the escape of our Richard the First from the iron durance of his prison here, appears to me infinitely more like one.

As soon as our neat comfortable breakfast was ended, we descended from what I think, from its size and pleasantness, must have been the apartment of the lady abbess, to the court-yard of the half-ruinous mansion, and by the active and good-humored assistance of the whole family we were soon in a condition to scale the castled crag, to reach which was the object of our enterprise. Two or three huge baskets were prepared, containing all that was needful for a mountain meal, and given in charge to the son of our host and the most perfect Diana of a country-girl that I ever saw. Bare-legged to the knee, with one basket balanced on her beautiful head, and another carried in her hand, as if it had been a light quiver of feathered arrows, she strode on with a free and active pace before the party. For some time the way led along the village street; then, turning suddenly at right angles to the river, it took us along a stony glen that brought us to the base of the almost precipitous slope which leads to the fortress of Durenstein. . . .

On the summit of this barren hill rises a shapeless rugged mass of rock, and it is on this that the keep of the castle is built; the rest of the edifice is on much lower ground, hanging, as it were, on the declivity that slopes towards the town; and it was probably in some chamber of this lower part that the royal prisoner was confined, which would certainly place him within reach of the voice of his minstrel I can now more easily believe, than at the time it was told me on the river, that Blondel's voice made itself heard from a turreted building at the foot of the mountain; for a part of the fortress hangs so completely over it, that it is easy to conceive the possibility of distinguishing an air in the stillness of night from the one point to the other.

Of this lower portion of the building, however, nothing now remains but the foundations, and here and there fragments of the walls, just sufficient to enable one to trace its outline. The keep itself is but a tottering roofless skeleton, yet still enough of it remains to give some notion of its architecture. There are one or two groinings of arches left, and one or two capitals of pillars in what was probably a little chapel. In one place are some faint remains of fresco painting on the walls, with remnants of an inscription, but too much obliterated to be legible. . . .

From the place I have chosen as my arm-chair and my writing-table I look down upon a chasm, on either side of which rise enormous masses of dark granite, in forms so strangely grotesque, that they look more like the wild carving of some savage sculptor than the

work of nature. From the river we mistook many of the isolated pinnacles with which the mountain is bristled for relics of gigantic fortifications; but now we find them to be more vast than any work of man. Nature seems kindly to have guarded the recesses of this cruel region by these threatening crags, as if on purpose to warn man from entering among them to seek a resting-place. But it was no resting-place that the artificer of yon dismal fortress sought; it was torture, anguish, and despair for which he was preparing; and, if his purpose were to find a spot where these could most surely be brought to perfection, he sought it well. . . .

Having explored the scanty remnant of the castle, some with more, and some with less intrepidity . . . for there is such ticklish treading about it, that no carpet dame, nor carpet knight either, would do well to attempt the adventure that we have performed . . . but having completed it, the party separated by agreement till the hour of dinner; each one, according to the law made and provided for such occasions by our travelling code, to dispose of the interval as may best please his or her fancy. The three sketchers, however, seem all attracted to nearly the same spot; T— has

darted off to explore the mountain far and near, and I am seated to my heart's content with shade, ruin, and rocks, all contributing to my enjoyment.

FRANCES TROLLOPE
Vienna and the Austrians, 1838

The reign of Emperor Francis Joseph I, which spanned the years from 1848 to 1916, was one of the longest —and some say the most glorious—in history. Last of the hereditary Habsburg monarchs to hold court at the twin capitals of Vienna and Budapest, the emperor by his very person welded together the improbable and fractious elements that made up the far-flung Dual Monarchy of Austria-Hungary. Living largely hidden from the public eye and emerging only on official occasions, Francis Joseph was naturally a target of gossip and the subject of books offering backstage glimpses of his monarchy. Henri de Weindel wrote one such book, mining his information from an anonymous "person of considerable rank at court." The result was a novelized romance laced with fact, and although it was published a full two years before the emperor's death in 1916, it dripped nostalgia for a

147

golden era obviously on the wane. In one chapter we are witness to the ceremonious arrival of Elizabeth of Bavaria, the emperor's cousin and future empress.

Drawn up in rough array along the bank of the Danube lines of peasantry, men and women, were gazing anxiously upstream. Then men, picturesquely clad in short jackets, tight breeches, and little round felt hats with turned-up brims, manoeuvred among groups of women whose shawl head-dresses terminated in wide stiff wings upon their necks. Suddenly a cry burst forth, ran along the ranks, and broke out into a roar: "Here they are! here they are!" Beating the water with a wheel on either side, a steamboat came into view, cutting a white trail of foam through the swirling blue waters. Already could be read in shining gold letters on the prow the name "Francis-Joseph." At a distance from the gathering of peasantry a fleecy cloud of smoke shot out, pierced by a ball of flame, and a loud report rent the air. A movement was seen on board the steamer, and a woman's figure, tall and slim, was observed to hurry forwards to the ship's nettings. In the interval between two salutes a volley of cheering went up from the banks, and the little hats waved in the peasants' hands. The slight figure responded with graceful acknowledgments.

She had been sitting in a dream, her eyes lost in space, on the hurricane-deck of the "Francis-Joseph," but at the first sound she had leapt quickly to her feet, crying: "What is happening? What is it?"

Undisturbed in his calm repose, and without ceasing to puff lazily at his huge pipe, the Duke Maximilian of Bavaria replied: "They are the subjects of your new Empire welcoming their future Empress."

"Their respect for me is shown in rather violent fashion, don't you think, father?"

The cheers from the river-bank grew louder and louder as the steamer came on. Elisabeth, whose bright hair shone brighter still in the sunlight, watched with amusement now the picturesque scene before her eyes. The Duchess Ludovica broke in: "Their cheers are for you, my daughter; you must acknowledge them."

Elisabeth, with a docility not devoid of pride, bowed gracefully. On the river-bank there was a perfect frenzy of joy. The "Francis-Joseph" steamed majestically on its way, while the cries of the peasants furnished a strident accompaniment to the thundering

bass of the cannons.

Gradually all the uproar died away in the distance.

"Where are we now?" asked Elisabeth.

"Near Linz, one of the chief towns of your new Empire, madame," answered the Duke Maximilian.

His words stirred the young girl's heart, for they recalled to her that romantic encounter in the park at Possenhofen, and it was with a softening of her voice that she replied:

"Madame? Not yet!"

"Oh, very soon. . . ."

"Three days off," said the Duchess. "In three days you will be Empress of Austria and Queen of Hungary."

"Queen of Hungary! I do not know why, but somehow that title is dearer to me."

"Take my advice," interrupted the Duke, "and don't mention that too loud in the presence of your husband."

Elisabeth was about to ask why, but she stood between two dreams—yesterday's and to-morrow's—and so she suffered herself to be lulled by the ship's gentle rocking, closed her eyes, and sank back into delicious self-communings.

At Linz, the capital of Upper Austria, while the cheering broke out again on both banks of the river, a gorgeously-clad officer stepped on board. It was the Emperor come to meet his *fiancée*, or, rather, it was not the Emperor, but Francis-Joseph the lover, offering his heart to the beautiful girl of Possenhofen. The official welcome, the Emperor's visit to the Duchess Elisabeth, was to take place next day, April 22nd, 1854, at the gates of Vienna.

HENRI DE WENDEL
*Behind the Scenes at the Court
of Vienna*, 1914

As longtime valet de chambre to Francis Joseph I, Eugen Ketterl was well placed to observe the emperor's private side. Years after Francis Joseph's death, the valet remembered his employer in a memoir that bordered on hagiography and characterized in glowing terms the man behind the public facade—a man who could be imperious and stern with those of high rank yet kindly and considerate to his servants. Part of the valet's job was to accompany Francis Joseph on state visits. What follows is Ketterl's account of the emperor's 1896 trip down the Danube to Orsova at the Iron Gate, where a new ship channel, rendering passable an especially hazardous stretch of the river, was opened with great fanfare by three reigning monarchs.

At the end of September 1896 we travelled to Roumania, being accompanied from Orsova onward by King Carol. Our Emperor was an intimate friend of King Carol and of the Poetess-Queen, Carmen Sylva, and the King had been His Majesty's guest in Vienna only a month before.

Probably gratitude on the part of the Roumanian King had been a factor in the proposed visit, for when it had not appealed to many of the foreign powers to see a Hohenzollern on the throne of Roumania, our Emperor had come warmly to the support of Karl of Hohenzollern, who had then been crowned. And now, in order to show other nations that Austria-Hungary looked upon the Kingdom of Roumania as an equal great power, His Majesty decided to pay an official visit, accompanied by a large suite, to the King Carol who had in actual fact made his new country great. An excellent opportunity offered when on the 25th September, 1897, the Danube Channel was opened at Orsova. Here, at the Iron Gate, numberless reefs, rocks and points barred the river passage at low water, and already two thousand years before the Romans under the Emperors Trajan and Tiberius had tried to make the dangerous place navigable. In 1833 Count Stephen Szechenyi worked energetically on the question, but it was 1884 before an international company, backed by the necessary capital, took the execution of the project properly in hand; and then it took fourteen years to complete the work. Now, with great pomp and ceremony, the "free" Danube was to be declared open by Emperor Francis Joseph, King Carol of Roumania and King Alexander of Serbia. Never in living memory had the little town of Orsova seen such a number of visitors, come from all directions in order to be present at this splendid spectacle. Dense crowds of Serbian, Hungarian, Bulgarian and Roumanian citizens lined the banks to view the ship carrying the Emperor, the King and the great nobles and statesmen. During the night of the 25th to the 26th September there shone reflected in the Danube's mirror-like surface also the splendid white steamer *Franz*

Josef I, escorted by a gunboat and the monitor *Körös.* The royal ship was followed by two others, carrying the high dignitaries of State, Church and Army, with other officials. The tug *Vaskapu* towed the royal steamer, whilst the *Radetzky* and the *Srinyi,* with the members of the European Danube Commission and the Inter-Parliamentary Conference on board, brought up the rear. A cable stretched from shore to shore represented the "last obstacle," and now from the poop of the royal vessel this too was set aside. Simultaneously on both banks cannon and guns thundered, and the glad shouts of the assembled people rang out. On the royal steamer the three monarchs raised their champagne-filled glasses, drinking together to the welfare and prosperity of their peoples and lands.

Eugen Ketterl
*The Emperor Francis Joseph I:
An Intimate Study,* 1930

It was not until the nineteenth century that Ottoman hegemony over the middle and lower Danube, stretching from the Black Sea through Hungary, was finally broken. From the sixteenth century onward, the Turks had ruled most of the Danube as corrupt despots, sometimes threatening the very gates of Vienna itself. It is no surprise, therefore, that nationalistic writers from Eastern Europe and the Balkans assailed the Ottoman presence and pressed liberation struggles against the hated invaders. One of these was Mór Jókai (1825–1904), a prominent Hungarian author who had taken part in the Kossuth revolt of 1848–49 and who later settled down to writing historical novels. In doing so he turned for his themes to the centuries-old Turkish rule over Hungary. Jókai's account of a grisly deed that was perpetrated by Turks in seventeenth-century Budapest is almost certainly an exaggeration of historical fact.

In the middle of the 17th century, there lived in Istanbul, capital of the Ottoman Empire, a white slave trader, named Hadzi Baba, who had heard from insiders in the Sultan's court that a huge Army was being assembled against Vienna and would be encamped at Buda, the center of Ottoman-occupied Hungary. Seeing a good opportunity, he packed his best merchandise—the most beautiful girls from all over the world—into a luxurious barge, guarded by eunuchs and decorated with Chinese silks, Persian rugs, and Venetian laces. Then he sailed out from Istanbul via the Bosphorus to the Black Sea and from there on the Danube river up to Buda, which is now a part of Budapest.

The wonderful boat caused a stir; all the Ottoman officials wanted to see its precious cargo. But Pasha Hassan, the *vezir* [governor] of Buda, ordered an embargo until he could select some of the girls for himself. He sent his confidant, Bey Yiffim, to Hadzi with that strict order and for a report. Hadzi kissed Yiffim's hand with servility and—just to show what a man he was—slapped the face of the eunuch on duty.

When they entered the richly decorated salon, Yiffim could not believe his eyes. There were eleven fine ladies, all transparently dressed, singing, plucking instruments, and playing games with each other.

"You must have robbed Paradise!" marveled Yiffim with a laugh.

"They are all my products. I nurtured them," said Hadzi. "I buy the girls when they are very young and adaptable. That way they can remember neither their parents nor their childhood and will stay joyful, loving, and desirable. Bought when they were older, they would recall their families, or maybe their lovers, cry all the time, and wither quickly."

Yiffim nodded in approval while Hadzi continued: "Each of them will cost 500 golden dinars, but this price is just for you. For others the price is double."

Pretending to listen with interest, Yiffim looked around, expecting something else, another surprise. Suddenly he moved to a corner, pushed aside the curtain, and found standing there a girl in a light, white wool caftan that covered her body. Yiffim watched her, petrified. Never in his life had he seen such a beauty. "You bastard!" he shouted, turning to Hadzi. "You wanted to deprive me of your best piece, a real *huri* [angel] kidnapped from Heaven."

"Oh no!" protested Hadzi. "It would be better if you would forget her. She is not for you . . ."

With an angry wave to Hadzi, Yiffim ordered the girl to drop the caftan, which she did with grace. She stood now nude and Yiffim was speechless.

"What is the price?" he asked after a while.

"My lord, she is not for you, believe me," answered Hadzi in a sad voice.

Yiffim bellowed: "What did you say, you man-headed dog? You dare to suppose that I do not have enough money to buy this girl? I am here on behalf of Hassan, the great vezir of Buda, a trustworthy friend and the first servant of the Sultan, whose habit it is to pay twice the price which is asked him. . . . If someone asks 1,000 golden dinars, he pays 2,000. . . . You should ask for this girl 10,000 golden dinars. If less, I will count the difference by the strokes of my whip on your bare soles." He raised his whip . . .

"You must understand me," begged Hadzi. "It is not the money that bothers me, but the spell . . . I would gladly give her to you for 100 golden dinars. Understand me, please! This girl. . . ."

Yiffim turned around and asked the girl whether she could sing. The girl reached for her mandolin and started to sing in a way that was out of this world.

Hadzi talked on in desperation: "This girl has already had five masters; all came to a tragic end. Poison. The dagger. A beheading. A silk cord from the court—gracious call for suicide. Strangulation. Wherever she goes, there is tragedy, sudden death, or unhappiness. No, do not take her!"

Yiffim was unmoved. He grabbed the girl, covered her with his own cloak, and, before leaving, asked Hadzi, "What is her name?"

"Azraële . . . a devilish name, and she deserves it." Then with a vibrating voice, he shouted after Yiffim, "Allah is my witness that I told you everything!"

On the third evening after Yiffim had taken the girl for Hassan, Hadzi was sitting on the deck of his barge, absorbed by the beauty of the Danube in the full moon. Further up he saw covered boats crossing the river in the direction of Margaret's Island. Suddenly he heard terrible, heartbreaking shrieks which were repeated rhythmically as one boat disappeared after the other in the silence followed by the screams. When the last shriek had ceased and the last boat had disappeared into the shadows of the shore, a beautiful voice arose from the hanging rose garden overlooking the Danube that belonged to Pasha Hassan, the *vezir* of Buda. The romantic song with its triumphant color was carried by the silver river.

Next morning Yiffim visited Hadzi and for almost an hour they sat in silence, sipping sherbet and smoking their pipes. Then Hadzi spoke: "Last night I saw boats crossing the river. And I heard terrible shrieks."

Yiffim said nothing. He just puffed and sipped. When he took his leave, he said stoically: "Those were the favorite harem girls of Pasha Hassan. They were stuffed into leather sacks and dumped into the Danube. . . ."

Hadzi shook his head, which meant in Turkish in those days that the whole tragedy was foreseeable.

MÓR JÓKAI
Ottoman Rule over Hungary, c. 1900

Richard Bright, an English physician, journeyed farther down the Danube than most early nineteenth-century tourists, and he eventually reached Walachia in what is now Romania. Bright spent much of his trip observing the colorful sights of Hungary's twin cities, Buda and Pesth—which people had not yet begun to call by their merged name. He later recorded his impressions in a travel narrative that characterized Hungary's capital as a stately yet bustling entrepôt, a polyglot center of commerce, culture, and government. Spanning the Danube at Budapest was the city's famous bridge; it held as much fascination for Bright more than 150 years ago as the city's modern, post-World War II bridges hold for tourists today.

Pesth and Buda, or, as it is otherwise called, Ofen, form almost one city, which is the capital of Hungary. They are separated by the Danube, here seen in all its majesty, over which is an easy communication by a bridge formed of forty-seven large boats, united by chains and covered with planks. The length of the bridge is nearly three hundred yards, and it is so constructed that two or three boats, with their planks and railings, may at any time be removed; and every morning and evening, at stated hours, the vessels and the rafts of timber which navigate or float down the Danube, are permitted to pass. At the approach of winter, however, large bodies of ice render it necessary to remove the bridge entirely; and for a period no communication exists between the two banks of the Danube, till the whole is so completely frozen as to afford a secure passage over the ice. . . .

Buda, the seat of the Hungarian Government, and the residence of the Palatine, contains 30,000 inhabitants. Its situation is on the right bank of the Danube, commanding and majestic. The extensive fortress, which occupies a high rock, contains the palaces of the Palatine, and of several Hungarian Nobles, the public arsenal and theatre, with many churches and streets, forming within itself a complete town. Round the foot of this rock, and along the side of the river, runs a street, while others, with gardens, surround it in different directions, and clothe the side of a second rocky eminence called the Blocksberg, which hangs over the river at a short distance to the south, and on which the new Observatory is constructed.

Pesth, the Transacincum of the Romans, occupies the left bank of the river. It is the seat of commerce, and contains nearly 33,000 inhabitants. It is built upon a plain, where it extends itself more and more every day, and is one of the very few towns upon the continent which seems to have suffered little during the late periods of disturbance. Besides the inn at which I lodged, several very extensive buildings were in progress; and, although we are not struck by any magnificence, we are certainly gratified by a considerable display of good streets and handsome houses, besides many churches and buildings belonging to different religious orders, each generally adorned with two steeples. . . .

The amusements of Pesth and Buda differ but little from those of the chief German towns. The theatres have been already mentioned. There are many coffeehouses, which are frequented in the evenings; and several public gardens, to which the people resort. A walk, sheltered by trees, along the western ramparts of Buda, overlooking the mountains and the vineyards, has long been the favourite place of assemblage when the weather is fine; and a similar parade has been lately formed on that bank of the Danube on which Pesth is placed. During the Carnival the usual festivities prevail; splendid public balls are held twice a week

in each of these towns, besides a great number of private assemblies, at which declamation is admitted as a favourite amusement; and, as the Palatine countenances the entertainments, and many of the Hungarian nobility make it a pride to support their establishments in their own capital, considerable vivacity is maintained in places of public resort. The two places in the vicinity of the town, to which the inhabitants chiefly withdraw, in order to enjoy, for a few hours, the refreshment of the country, are the garden of Graf Ortzy, and the spot which is denominated the Forest. The former is about three miles distant from the town. It is a garden and shrubbery, laid out with taste, and liberally opened by the proprietor to all who visit it. The garden is handsome, and the views of Ofen add greatly to its beauty. The Forest is rather a projected than a finished pleasure-ground. It was intended to convert a large piece of land, not very fertile in its nature, into a beautiful labyrinth of shrubs and flowers. Many trees were planted; and, though the object was never completed, the Forest still serves as an occasional excursion in the summer afternoon.

RICHARD BRIGHT
*Travels from Vienna through
Lower Hungary,* 1818

Son of a worker and idealistic member of the Hungarian Communist party, Attila József (1905–37) was also one of Hungary's greatest modern poets. Not surprisingly, József wrote poetry that gave voice to the frustrations and squalor of Hungarian working-class life between the two world wars. In the following work the poet is found sitting beside the Danube at Budapest, musing on Hungary's "turbulent, wise and great" river of eternity.

As I sat on the bottom step of the wharf,
A melon-rind flowed by with the current;
Wrapped in my fate I hardly heard the chatter
Of the surface, while the deep was silent.
As if my own heart had opened its gate:
The Danube was turbulent, wise and great.

Like a man's muscles when hard at his toil,
Hammering, digging, leaning on the spade,
So bulged and relaxed and contracted again
Each single movement, each and every wave.
It rocked me like my mother for a time
And washed and washed the city's filth and grime.

And the rain began to fall but then it stopped
Just as if it couldn't have mattered less,

And like one watching the long rain from a cave,
I gazed away into the nothingness.
Like grey, endless rain from the skies overcast,
So fell drably all that was bright: the past.

But the Danube flowed on. And the sprightly waves
In playful gaiety laughed at me again,
Like a child on his prolific mother's knee,
While other thoughts were racing through her brain.
They trembled in Time's flow and in its wake,
Like in a graveyard tottering tomb-stones shake.

I am he who for a hundred thousand years
Has gazed on what he now sees the first time.
One brief moment and, fulfilled, all time appears
In a hundred thousand forbears' eyes and mine.
I see what they could not for their daily toil,
Killing, kissing as duty dictated,
And they, who have descended into matter,
See what I do not, if truth be stated.

We know of each other like sorrow and joy,
Theirs is the present and mine is the past;
We write a poem, they're holding my pencil
And I feel them and recall them at last. . . .
I am the Forbear who split and multiplied,
Shaped my father and mother into whole,
My father and mother then in turn divide
And so I have become one single soul.

I am the world, all that is past exists:
Men are fighting men with renewed anguish.
Dead conquerors ride to victory with me
And I feel the torment of the vanquished.
Arpad and Zalan, Werböczy and Dözsa,
Turks and Tartars, Slovaks, Rumanians
Fill my heart which owes this past a calm future
As our great debt, today's Hungarians.

I want to work. For it is battle enough
Having a past such as this to confess.
In the Danube's waves past, present and future
Are all-embracing in a soft caress.
The great battle which our ancestors once fought
Resolves into peace through the memories,
And to settle at last our communal affairs
Remains our task and none too small it is.

ATTILA JÓZSEF
"By the Danube," 1936

The Danube seemed, near Belgrade, an expanse of waters which would have afforded ample space for the whole of the British navy. We had scarcely left Semendria behind us when the river became still wider, resembling indeed a vast lake, sufficient, as to superficial extent at least, to contain all the navies of the world. It was here in every respect a truly magnificent object. The more I became acquainted with this noble river, the greater was my astonishment that it was so little known to Europe, and hitherto so rarely made use of for the purposes of commerce. Just as the sun was on the decline, flinging his last rays on the tranquil mirror beneath us, the Tyrolese crowded on deck and favoured us with several of their national songs, which they performed with infinite spirit. It was the last time I was to hear them, as we expected to arrive at night at Vipalanka, where they were to debark on their way to Transylvania.

After passing Kubin, we perceived the commencement of several groups of islands, which, however beautiful in themselves, diminish the majestic character the Danube would otherwise have maintained the whole way from Semendria to Moldava. They occasionally divide the waters into two or three rivers in appearance; none of which, however, can be considered as insignificant. The main current which runs by the Hungarian bank retains uniformly much of the general grandeur of the parent flood. These islands are densely wooded with osiers and evergreen shrubs, which afford a safe refuge for water-fowl of every description. Wild ducks and geese frequently rose in clouds one above another in the sky, winging their way towards their island homes. Now and then a solitary eagle sailed through the firmament. . . .

The unruffled surface of the Danube reflected the whole canopy of the sky, and gave back in softened tones the saffron, ruby, and purple lines of fire, which still glowed in the west. The image of the departing sun was lengthened in the waters, where it appeared like a long perpendicular column of light. This optical delusion was the more striking, as the part of the Danube in which we had now arrived was, in fact, little better than a series of shallows, through which we were steering our course with the utmost difficulty.

As soon as the sun went down, the night became rapidly so dark, that I know not how we should have contrived to pursue our way, had not some fields of stubble on the left bank been accidentally set on fire. The flame threw its light far along the river, and materially assisted the helmsman to keep his track. Here and there, among the inlets of the islands on the opposite shore, lights also were visible, proceeding from fires kindled for the purposes of cooking, by fishermen or fowlers, whose little boats were moored in the neighbourhood. Vast pillars of smoke moved now and then over the blazing stubbles, assuming the most fantastic shapes; sometimes, as they apparently flitted along the bank, they might have been painted by an imaginative spectator as the spirits of the Danube. . . .

So abrupt and frequent were the windings of the Danube, amid the beauteous hills which form its banks below the narrow gorge of rocks above described, that often, on looking back we saw no trace of the direction by which we had come; nor, on looking before us, could we discern by what course we were to proceed. We seemed to be shut in on all sides, as within a mountain lake, from which there was no apparent egress, until, by turning a little cape, we found ourselves in another and another lake, in succession. We left this charming scenery behind us, on approaching the rapids of the Danube, where its bed is wholly composed of rough rocks, sometimes starting up in masses nearly to the surface of the river, sometimes forming a wall, running across from bank to bank, and producing a perceptible fall in the current. We were warned of the danger to be encountered on passing these rapids, by the hoarse murmur of the waters which we had heard at a distance. The obstacles which the river met in its course produced considerable undulations on its surface, amounting now and then to waves, on which our bark was hurried away, notwithstanding all the efforts of our rowers, and dashed against the rocks. Had our boat not been a very strong one, or had the impulse been somewhat stronger, we should probably have been wrecked among these rapids, owing chiefly to the unskilfulness of our people, as well as the ludicrous state of alarm

The whole of this narrow passage amongst the rocks was curious and highly romantic. A little beyond the petrified mill, on the opposite side, we beheld a perfect outline of an immense lion, crouching; the head, the eyes, the mouth, and the paws, were as correctly delineated on the naked stone, as if they had been drawn by the hand of an artist. A cluster of rocks, somewhat further on, assumed all the appearance of the ruins of a cathedral, with its towers and ivied walls, and Gothic windows and gates. The effect of this pile was remarkably picturesque, as it rose on an eminence above a mass of green foliage, which seemed to conceal the lower parts of the cathedral.

MICHAEL QUIN
A Steam Voyage down the Danube, 1836

in which their ignorance involved them.

The banks again assumed a wild rocky character, and approached so near each other, that, when the river is full, the volume of waters which rush through that space must be terrific. As it was, we were constantly rubbing on the bottom, and might have walked almost dry-footed on ledges which extended quite across the stream. The boat was literally carried over these ledges, as there was not water enough to float it. Our patron repeatedly told us that he, though seventy-three years old, had never known the Danube so low as it was upon that occasion. In the almost perpendicular wall which rose on our right, there was a singular *lusus naturae* on a gigantic scale—it was the complete figure of a water-mill and mill-house petrified, and slightly crushed by an enormous rock which had fallen upon it from the higher precipices. The face of the superincumbent mass presented the figure of a monk preaching from a pulpit; and it only required the existence of a legend, to induce a superstitious mind to believe, that the "miller and his men" had been notorious criminals—that the monk had come to reprove them—and that while he was still vainly exhorting them to repentance, the living scene was suddenly transformed into stone.

Pock-marked with rapids, shoals, sandbars, and whirlpools, the Danube is at once a navigator's nightmare and sightseer's dream. Between Orsova and Turnu-Severin, Romania, stands the river's celebrated Iron Gate, a narrow gorge that was once a swirling ship's graveyard but is now freely passable thanks to the Djerdap Dam, jointly administered by Romania and Yugoslavia. When the history-conscious Romanian writer Alexandru Vlahuță passed through the Iron Gate at the beginning of the twentieth century, the gorge was still as the Romans had found it many centuries before. In a travel book that won him a top prize from the Romanian Academy of Literature in 1902, Vlahuță painted a lively portrait of the region.

We are approaching the threshold of the "Cataracts" . . . [where] the Danube begins its angry rush. Whirling waves struggle from one bank to the other. . . . Here the water sinks, there it swells, grows, and howls, foaming and beating against the hidden reefs.

Our ship sails slower, more cautiously. Four people stay at the helm. Both captains stand watch on deck, always staring ahead. Now we are crossing the "Cataracts." The Danube roars louder. Eyes closed, one imagines himself in the woods during a terrible storm. Beneath the waves, innumerable stone arms stretch upward, ready to catch the ship and break it to pieces at the slightest mistake. Here, under this eddy, is the junction of the Balkans with the Carpathian Mountains. Above their clenched fists, the Danube furiously hurls itself, noisily breaking the final constraints that stand in its way. In the bustle of this clash between the two giants, it seems that each wave is crying, each rock is moving.

Suddenly the stream slips by the rugged obstacle and spreads out like a sheet. The fight, the terrible fight between the two Titans, is over. Defeated, the mountains give way. The horizon opens. . . .

But what a distance the Danube has traveled, and how hard it has fought in order to reach this point! It has had to cleave the mountains to dig its rock-bed across the Carpathians. But ultimately the river triumphs, and the "Iron Gates" open before the eternal strength of its waves.

Now the roaring ceases. Victorious, the water rests between the banks, relieved, smooth as a mirror. The Carpathians push their wood-shrouded hills to the north. Strange rocks raise their bald heads from the green thicket, as if desiring once more to view the moving, irresistible flood. . . .

From Varciorova, a railroad rims the riverbank to Turnu-Severin. . . . Larger than before, the Danube cuts a bend in the Romanian ground. . . . Up on a tree-covered hill [the town of Turnu-Severin] reveals its big white houses covered with red-tiled roofs. Dense black smoke rises from factory chimneys. We hear from afar the noise made by big factory machinery, while on the shore we see crowds swarming on the wharf as if at a fair.

This place is full of ancient memories. Eighteen centuries ago Roman legions came here to found a new nation in the wasted fields of old Dacia. Here the Roman Emperor Lucius Septimius Severus erected the eastern shield of his Empire, the so-called "Severian Camp." Even today we can see vestiges like Sever's Tower in the town's public garden, situated high on a terrace with a beautiful view of the Danube.

The capital of Oltenia Province also was once here, the seat of the famous Bans of the Severin, whose origin fades into an era predating even the founding of Romania. Archaeological digs in this neighborhood have unveiled antique walls, sculptured figures, tools, and Roman coins—scattered memories of a world full of heroes that brought to the Walachian Plain the light, the language, and the power of the most glorious empire that ever existed.

What fantastic artifacts Trajan's Roman legion-

naires left here! We still can recognize their steps carved into the mountain paths. Everything here they conquered. The rocks gave in and let them pass. The waters also submitted to the shadow and sound and strength of the first bridges ever to span them. Even the Danube—the magnificent and impetuous Danube —was tamed, finally surrendering to the soldiers of Rome.

ALEXANDRU VLAHUȚĂ
Picturesque Romania, c. 1900

In April, 1876, Bulgarian revolutionary Christo Botev and two hundred of his followers boarded the Austrian Danube steamer Radetzki, *commandeered the boat at a Romanian port, and then headed downstream to Bulgaria. Their arrival touched off a brief but costly insurrection against the Turks that left 16,000 Bulgarians dead—among them Botev—but is nonetheless recognized as a valiant chapter in the nation's tortured history. Ivan Vazov subsequently enshrined Botev's Danube crossing in the following poem.*

Quiet and white, the Danube rippled and cheerfully
    murmured
And the *Radetzki* proudly sailed upon the golden
    waves.
But when the shores of Kozloduy appeared,
A horn sounded on board and a flag unfurled.
Brave young Bulgarian men lined up,
Lion badges on their foreheads, fire in their eyes.
And before them their young leader proudly stood.
Sabre drawn, he addressed the ship's captain:
"I am a Bulgarian commander and these are my men;
We fly to shed blood for freedom today.
We fly to help Bulgaria,
To liberate her from tyranny.
Give us this ship; do it forthwith
So we may cross to our native shores."
When the captain—a true German—refused to obey,
Botev, frowning, exclaimed in a thunderous voice:
"This I demand! I don't beg! All of you are captives
    now
And my will is obeyed when I'm in command!
Listen, today my people are dying, fighting the hated
    foe,
So swiftly sail this ship on to Bulgaria!"

His voice struck terror as he spoke,
And the German, pale and frightened, obeyed his
    command.
In haste he steered the ship toward its destination,
And the Danube was lively, in a joyous mood.
For a long time it hadn't borne
The brave Bulgarian men it loves.
The company broke into a war song
And the lion banner proudly waved.
As the ship approached the beloved shore,
Botev bared his head and spoke once more:
"Forward brothers! This is where we land,
Kiss the earth we've come to die on!"
And in joyful ecstasy 'round the lion flag
All fell to their knees on the sacred shore.
"Brothers!" their leader thundered,
"Soon the people meet us with joy!
Soon we will greet the Balkan mountains with fire,
Soon begin our bloody battles with the Turks!
Untried we are in war and our numbers are few,
Yet our hearts are aflame, yearning for battle!
The Turks soon will feel our awesome might
Our shield will be justice; the lion, our captain!"
A stirring call echoed 'round the whole valley—
"Long live Bulgaria! To the evil tyrant—death!"

IVAN VAZOV
"Radetzki," c. 1880

The Danube delta, with its vast expanses of reed and water, its unspoiled marshy wastelands, and its huge reserves of fish, is witness to the final act of the river's drama, for here the mighty waters empty into the Black Sea. When John Marriner helped film the lower Danube on assignment for the BBC in 1968, he traveled upriver from the Black Sea to Vienna; thus the delta was the first and not the last of the river's wonders that he explored. On his way, he came upon a band of expatriate Russian "Old Believers," who now live quietly along the Danube's shores as fishermen, largely forgotten by the world.

We lunched *en passage*, the bright sunshine streaming down on us. It was all very pleasing. Gradually, I gained confidence in the river. It was well signposted and it was perfectly clear which signs meant "Moor here," "Anchor here," "Don't anchor here," "Turn around here" and "No overtaking here." Our British chart seemed dead accurate and all the lights were as marked on it. Occasionally, and especially at any bends, training banks of stone had been built out into the river to help it keep its course. The end of each of these was marked by a white ball and we kept well away from them and the swirling whirlpools they set up. Just below Milla 13, I saw a monument which had been put up to those who completed the Sulina Canal in 1898 but I could not read the inscription on it, which seemed blackened and possibly defaced.

A moment later and we had turned sharp right into a remaining arm of the Old Danube. The depths below us decreased alarmingly to some five feet or so, but quickly increased again and we found ourselves to our great delight in a charming winding river—no longer a fast rushing canal stream—with clear still waters deepening to some 20 feet beneath us. The whole of the Sulina arm had once, I supposed, been like this until the Sulina Ship Canal was completed. It must have been difficult for ocean-going ships to get around some of the bends. Since the canal was built, the Old Danube here had retired, by-passed and forgotten, into its medieval shell, but still welcoming visitors with recollections of its great days. On the banks, peasants were starting to cut the reeds which grew everywhere for thousands of acres. The main harvest would come in September/October, when the green reeds, already going brown, would be shipped up to Braila and Tulcea to the factories which turned them into paper, cellulose, building material, glycerine and various kinds of alcohol! It was only in recent times that these modern uses had been discovered—until then, the riches of the rushes had been reserved almost exclusively to roofs and fences.

Enchanted by our new surroundings, we dropped anchor for a swim. The pale brown water, warm on the top and cooler below, jolted me roughly back from the daily cares of travel in a strange country to a kinship with nature that soothed and pacified. What did it matter, I thought, as I floated gently in the Danube, whether we ever got to the Iron Gate, whether the BBC were pleased with our film, whether the Bulgarians would co-operate properly and whether indeed my boat survived the hazards of the torrent? The welcoming water lapped at my ears, the reeds sighed at the banks and high above the lark sang

sweetly in the eastern skies. I had been told in Constantsa that as many as 300 different species of bird nest in the Delta. Of these, 74 are non-Europeans who come here to hatch and rear their young before flying off to a warmer winter elsewhere, mostly to Africa. Among these one can list the wild duck, the swan, egrets, flamingoes and the most curious of all—the pelicans, scavengers of the Delta, who live in secret colonies which we hoped to discover. Of the fish, there are said to be some 60 different kinds, the most famous being, of course, the sturgeon, which sometimes reach a weight of 500 kilograms. Wolves, foxes and wild boar are among the more picturesque of the animals, though these are, I would say, limited by the relative smallness of the land available. The whole area of the Delta is estimated at about one thousand square miles, mostly consisting of swamps and marshes through which the river, heavy with silt, meanders towards the sea. When one considers that the northern Khilia arm, which accounts for about 67 per cent of the total water poured into the Black Sea, carries with it no less than 3,000 cubic feet of sediment per minute, it is small wonder that the entire Delta area is advancing yearly into the sea at an even greater rate than the estuary of the Rhone. Near the coast, the river subdivides into many lakes and abandoned channels, like the one in which I was floating,

all indicating how badly the area is drained. It is not easy to get about in the Delta unless you have a boat. There are, it is true, some tourist steamer services in the summer season, but there are few regular lines, except on the main channel between Tulcea and Sulina and Tulcea and St. George. . . .

Back aboard and dry, it was not long before we found ourselves off the *cherhana* at Milla 23, which is the name given, somewhat *faute de mieux*, to an altogether charming fishing village located at a point just 23 sea-miles up the Old Danube arm from the sea. Moored at the *cherhana* was a strange-looking motorship, the *Pinguin*. She was an ice-maker and we stopped to book a few bars for next morning. Across the river lay the main village, mostly a collection of thatched huts with reed fences separating one plot of tenuous land from another. With an anchor in mid-Danube, I put my stern to a rickety jetty, laid a gangway to it, and balanced myself ashore. We were in the Delta.

We all have only pleasant memories of this place. After dinner, we went ashore to the local inn, where there were a dozen or so men sitting. Women were scarcely to be seen, since the local attitude to women is only one better than in Turkey. A few hung around, however, on the outskirts of the group where their menfolk lorded it supreme. Tutu had already told me about how greatly vodka was enjoyed in this part of the world and we had wisely stowed a case aboard back in Constantsa. A bottle placed fair and square on the inn table worked wonders and before long we were being treated to a weirdly stirring selection of Russian singing.

For these people are not of true Romanian origin. They are the Lipoveni, a tribe of Russian expatriates who, in the time of Peter the Great's seventeenth-century reforms, decided that they were not of the same opinion as their Czar and took the long track south out of his domains. Calling themselves "the Old Believers," a name they still hold, the Lipoveni disapproved of the fashionable new translations of the gospels and all the wicked things, such as smoking, which the Czar was bringing about. Not for them such baubles, so off they went south through the lipo or lime forests of the Ukraine and arrived at last in and around the Danube Delta, where the name of Lipoveni, meaning a dweller in a lime forest, has ever since stuck to them. At first, their lack of razors caused them always to appear with beards; even when razors at last became available to them they kept the beards as a sign of their religion. Today, the younger men mostly shave, except the priests, but there are many older men who would never dream of abandoning their beards for all the vodka in Russia. I need hardly say that now everybody smokes! When they first arrived in the Delta, the Lipoveni were forced to fish to eat: now they are the traditional fishermen of the Delta and it is almost solely from this activity that they earn their present living. They claim that the phosphorus in the fish gives them excellent sight. This I really do not feel able to comment on, except to say that they always start fishing about half-past two in the morning, so at least their sight can be no worse than anyone else's! They are, of course, now all Romanian citizens—at least those who actually live in Romanian territory—but religiously they are organised under their Bishop Joseph, who resides at Braila in a street anomalously named 1st of May. Some 5,000 Lipoveni live in the Romanian part of the Delta, though it is estimated that there are a great many more in Russia along the banks of the River Pruth, one of the Danube's lower tributaries. They told me that their faith was their main interest in life (the religion is basically Russian Orthodox) with their food, work and ceremonies coming next. . . .

The village priest was a gentle and helpful man. We came across him at his solitary office one morning and he immediately, his prayers over, agreed to tell us all he knew of his sect and their strange lonely lives. He had a small son, with whom he was photographed in the churchyard, and a wife, a lady with a biting tongue, who tried to prevent him from helping us. The interior of his wooden church was covered with brightly painted ikons: the floors were bare, and when I saw where the floods came, I understood why. The village of Milla 23 stretched like a snake along one bank of the Old Danube, thatched house succeeding thatched house. . . . One of the most odd buildings in the village was a long, low, barn-like thatch-covered affair which we were told was an ice store. When the river ice broke up in March, the Lipoveni would gather the great hunks and fill the store with them. Protected from the weather, the ice would last for weeks, preserving fish against the arrival of the collecting boats and the ultimate appearance of the *Pinguin*.

JOHN MARRINER
Black Sea and Blue River, 1968

The River at a Glance

From its source deep in West Germany's Black Forest to its outlet on the Black Sea, the Danube River alternately slices, twists, and demurely glides for 1,776 miles across central and southeastern Europe. Some 1,600 of these miles are navigable, on the average, for ten-and-a-half ice-free months per year. The Danube drains a land mass of 315,000 square miles—slightly smaller than the combined land area of Texas and Arkansas. Among Europe's great rivers it ranks second to the Volga in both length and drainage area (Russia's major river is 2,293 miles long and drains 525,000 square miles). By contrast, the Rhine, Europe's most important and most heavily used commercial waterway, is only 820 miles long and has a 62,000-square-mile drainage area. Less than half the Danube's length, the Rhine carries more than double the Danube's river traffic. Statistically, the Danube is peerless on its continent in one category only: its average water volume of five thousand cubic yards per second far exceeds that of any other European river, giving its current impressive velocity and power. Yet the river is underdeveloped as a source of irrigation and hydroelectric power. The great stream's winding bed ingathers the waters of approximately three hundred tributaries, thirty-four of which are navigable and some of which—like the Sava and the Tisza—are themselves mighty rivers.

The entire Danube River basin may be divided into three distinguishable courses—the upper, middle, and lower Danubes—each roughly equal in length and each marked by unique physical features and somewhat differing ecosystems. The upper Danube extends for some six hundred miles from the river's twin sources—tiny Black Forest streams named the Brege and the Brigach—to a gorge located between the Alps and the Carpathians near Bratislava, Czechoslovakia, that is known as the Hungarian Gate. In this wild, hilly, and beautiful section, the Danube passes the Swabian and Franconian mountains and the Bavarian Plateau in Germany, then enters the Bohemian Forest in Austria; the river swells dramatically in size here, absorbing the outflows of such major tributaries as the Inn, Iller, Lech, Isar, Traun, Enns, and Morava rivers.

The middle Danube, which stretches from the Hungarian Gate to the Iron Gate near Turnu-Severin, Romania, flows through considerably more level terrain; in these reaches the river is characterized by low, widely separated banks. Rushing through a narrow gorge at Viségrad, Hungary, the Danube plunges due south into the vast, flat Hungarian Plain, an open expanse where the river becomes sluggish, deposits silt, and builds up numerous sandbars and islands. Farther on, major tributaries like the Drava, Tisza, and Sava replenish the attenuated Danube before it reaches the Iron Gate, a narrow, two-mile gorge in which the channel churns to a swirling froth. Today the Djerdap High Dam, built and jointly maintained by Romania and Yugoslavia, has tamed this notoriously dangerous river cataract and tapped its hydroelectric potential.

Beyond the Iron Gate lies the lower Danube. In this stretch the river moves across the Danubian and Walachian plains of Romania and Bulgaria, absorbs major tributaries including the Olt, Siret, and Prut rivers, and finally reaches the delta—the climax of its long journey. A reedy, marshy wasteland that presently covers some 4,299 square kilometers and is expanding seaward by eighty to one hundred feet annually, the Danube delta empties into the Black Sea via three "arms": the Kiliya, St. George, and Sulina channels. Only the last of these is navigable, maintained by constant dredging.

Although the Danube ranks as only the twenty-fourth longest river in the world, it holds a place of unique importance for European civilization. More than an inspiration for graceful waltzes—but always a home for great music—the Danube throughout much of recorded history has been a cultural crossroads, commercial highway, invasion route, buffer zone, and bloody battleground—between great empires, between Asia and Europe, between Moslem and Christian. Indeed, for millennia warrior peoples—among them Romans, Huns, Mongols, and Turks—traveled the Danube's banks hoping to carve out empires. These belligerents invariably failed—but not before depositing bits of culture and, more often, mountains of misery. In our century the Danube's commercial importance has grown steadily although it has never quite lived up to expectations, due as much to the problems of international regulation of the river as to those of navigating it. By the early 1970s the eight riparian nations plying the Danube shipped a total of only 2.7 million tons of freight annually (compared to 230 million tons on the Mississippi). Still, the economic well-being of many cities—including the three East European capitals of Vienna, Budapest, and Belgrade—is closely tied to the river's further development. Canals, either planned or completed, will eventually link the Danube to a Continent-wide inland waterway system. Since World War II, Soviet-style regimes have governed all but two riparian nations, and the Danube is now largely under Soviet domination. Thus the river carries on its tradition of dividing hostile worlds—this time the worlds of capitalism and communism. No less than yesterday's, today's Danube awaits an uncertain future.

The world's major rivers, ranked by length[1]	Length		Drainage area		Average discharge[2] at mouth cu. ft./sec. (000)	Delta area (sq. km.)	Source
	Miles	Kms.	Sq. Km. (000)	Sq. Mi. (000)			
Nile	4,132	6,650	1,293	3,349	100	20,228 (Egypt)	Lake Victoria (Uganda)
Amazon	4,000	6,437	2,722	7,050	7,500	Estuary (Brazil)	Andes (Peru)
Mississippi-Missouri	3,741	6,020	1,244	3,221	611	26,159 (USA)	Mississippi: Lake Itaska (Minn.) Missouri: Lake Sakakawea (N.D.)
Yenisey	3,442	5,540	996	2,580	614	2,460 (USSR)	Confluence of Bi-Khem and Ka-Khem Rivers (Siberia)
Yangtze	3,434	5,494	756	1,959	770	Estuary (China)	Tanglha Range (China)
Ob-Irtysh	3,362	5,410	1,149	2,975	441	2,849 (USSR)	Altai Mountains (USSR)
Yellow (Huang Ho)	3,011	4,845	288	745	116	1,940 (China)	Tsinghai Highlands (China)
Congo (Zaïre)	2,914	4,700	1,314	3,457	1,400	2,072 (Zaïre)	Katanga Plateau (Zaïre)
Amur	2,800	4,480	716	1,855	388	Estuary (USSR)	Confluence of Argun and Shilka Rivers (USSR–China)
Lena	2,734	4,400	961	2,490	547	25,900 (USSR)	Baikal Range (USSR)
Mackenzie	2,635	4,241	711	1,841	280	12,200 (Canada)	Great Slave Lake (Canada)
Niger	2,600	4,180	730	1,890	215	36,260 (Nigeria)	Fouta Djallon Mountains (Guinea)
St. Lawrence-Great Lakes	2,500	4,020	565	1,463	500	Estuary (Canada)	Lake Superior
Mekong	2,500	4,000	307	795	390	50,000 (S. Vietnam)	Tanglha Range (China)
Río de La Plata-Paraná-Paraguay	2,485	4,000	1,600	4,144	526	Estuary (Argentina)	Confluence of Grande and Paranaíba rivers (Brazil)
Murray-Darling	2,350	3,780	408	1,057	4*	——	Snowy Mountains (Australia)
Volga	2,293	3,690	525	1,360	80*	9,970 (USSR)	Valday Hills (USSR)
Zambezi	2,200	3,540	514	1,330	250	7,148 (Mozambique)	Northwest Zambia
Purus	2,100	3,400	89	231	——	——	Andes (Peru)
Madeira	2,082	3,350	386	997	——	——	Confluence of Beni and Mamoré rivers (Bolivia)
Rio Grande	1,885	3,040	172	445	.8*	——	San Juan Mountains (Colorado)
São Francisco	1,800	2,900	260	673	100		Serra da Canastra (Brazil)
Ganges-Brahmaputra	1,800	2,897	626	1,621	660	59,570 (Bangladesh)	Kumaun Highlands (India)
Indus	1,790	2,880	450	1,166	196	——	Kailas Range (Tibet)
Danube	1,776	2,850	315	816	218	4,299 (Romania)	Black Forest (W. Germany)
Tigris-Euphrates	1,700	2,740	430	1,114	51	——	Tigris: Lake Golcuk (Turkey) Euphrates: Confluence of Murat and Kara Rivers (Turkey)

[1] Source: expanded and modified from *Encyclopædia Britannica* (1974) except where otherwise indicated.

[2] Source: U.S. Geological Survey, 1964
* Indicates mean discharge expressed in cu. m./sec. (000)

Outlet	Countries of Passage	Major dams in the river system[3] (including tributaries)
Mediterranean Sea	Uganda, Sudan, Egypt	Egypt: Aswan
Atlantic Ocean	Peru, Colombia, Brazil	———
Gulf of Mexico	USA	USA: Fort Peck, Fort Randall, Garrison, Kingsley, Oahe, Tuttle Creek, Yellowtail
Kara Sea (Arctic Ocean)	USSR (Siberia)	———
East China Sea	China	———
Ob Bay (Kara Sea)	USSR (Siberia)	———
Gulf of Chihli (Yellow Sea)	China	———
Atlantic Ocean	Zaïre, Congo, Angola	———
Tatar Strait (Sea of Okhotsk)	USSR, China	———
Laptev Sea (Arctic Ocean)	USSR (Siberia)	———
Arctic Ocean	Canada	Canada: W.A.C. Bennett
Gulf of Guinea (Atlantic Ocean)	Guinea, Mali, Niger, Dahomey, Nigeria	———
Gulf of St. Lawrence (Atlantic Ocean)	Canada, USA	Canada: Manicouagan No. 5
South China Sea	China, Burma, Laos, Thailand, Cambodia, Vietnam	———
Atlantic Ocean	Brazil, Paraguay, Argentina	Brazil: Solteira Island
Encounter Bay (Indian Ocean)	Australia	Australia: Talbingo
Caspian Sea	USSR	USSR: Gorky, Ivankova, Saratov, Volga-22nd Congress, Volga-V.I. Lenin
Indian Ocean	Zambia, Angola, Rhodesia, Mozambique	Mozambique: Cabora Bassa; Rhodesia-Zambia: Kariba
Amazon River	Peru, Brazil	———
Amazon River	Bolivia, Brazil	———
Gulf of Mexico	USA, Mexico	USA: Cochiti
Atlantic Ocean	Brazil	———
Bay of Bengal	India, Bangladesh	———
Arabian Sea	Tibet (China), Pakistan, India	India: Bhakra, Beas Pakistan: Jari, Mangla, Tarbella
Black Sea	W. Germany, Austria, Czechoslovakia, Hungary, Yugoslavia, Bulgaria, Romania	Yugoslavia: Mratinje; Romania: Vidraru; Yugoslavia-Romania: Djerdap
Persian Gulf	Turkey, Syria, Iraq	Iraq: Bekhme; Turkey: Keban

[3] Source: U.S. Bureau of Reclamation (1969). This table lists major dams of at least 492 feet in height, or a total volume of embankment exceeding 20,000,000 cubic yards.

Selected Bibliography

Admiralty Naval Staff, Naval Intelligence Division. *A Handbook of the River Danube*. 1915–19.

Barraclough, Geoffrey. *The Origins of Modern Germany*. Oxford: Basil Blackwell, 1946.

Bushbeck, Ernst H. *Austria*. London: Oxford University Press, 1949.

Evans, Stanley G. *A Short History of Bulgaria*. London: Lawrence & Wishart, 1960.

Funk, Addie. *Legends, Vienna, and the Blue Danube*. Vienna: Knoch, 1955.

Gorove, Stephen. *Law and Politics of the Danube*. The Hague: M. Nijhoff, 1964.

Heer, Friedrich. *The Holy Roman Empire*. Translated by Janet Sondheimer. New York: F. A. Praeger, 1968.

Heppell, Muriel, and Singleton, F. B. *Yugoslavia*. London: E. Benn, 1961.

Hertz, Frederick. *The Economic Problem of the Danubian States*. London: V. Gollancz, 1947.

Kavka, František. *An Outline of Czechoslovak History*. Translated by Jarmila and Ian Milner. Prague: Orbis, 1960.

Leeper, Alexander W. A. *A History of Medieval Austria*. London: Oxford University Press, 1941.

Lengyel, Emil. *The Danube*. New York, Random House, 1939.
———. *1,000 Years of Hungary*. New York: John Day Company, 1958.

Lessner, Erwin. *The Danube*. Garden City: Doubleday & Company, 1961.

Montfort, Guy. *The Wild Danube*. Boston: Houghton Mifflin, 1963.

Popescu, Julian. *The Danube*. London: Oxford University Press, 1961.

Redlich, Josef. *Emperor Francis Joseph of Austria: A Biography*. New York: The Macmillan Company, 1929.

Seton-Watson, Robert William. *A History of the Roumanians: From Roman Times to the Completion of Unity*. Archon Books, 1963.

Stavrianos, Leften S. *The Balkans Since 1453*. New York: Rinehart, 1958.

Trost, Ernst. *Die Donau: Lebenslauf eines Stromes*. Vienna: F. Molden, 1968.

Wechsberg, Joseph. *Vienna, My Vienna*. New York: Macmillan, 1968.

Acknowledgments

The Editors would like to thank Imre Kovács, Liviu Floda, and Nicolas Pentcheff for their respective translations of excerpts from works by Mór Jókai, Alexandru Vlahută, and Ivan Vazov that appear in *The Danube in Literature*. The Editors also wish to express their appreciation to Marvin E. Newman for his creative photography and to Eva Bakos for her invaluable assistance in Vienna. In addition, the Editors would like to thank the following individuals and organizations:
Russell Ash, London
Austrian National Tourist Office, New York—Walter Czerney
Alexander Bakos, Vienna
Margot Granitsas, New York
Horizon Magazine, New York—Mary Sherman Parsons
Barbara Nagelsmith, Paris
Georgio Nimatallah, Milan
Lynn Seiffer, New York
United Nations Map Collection—Nathaniel O. Abelson
Sylvia Winsor, Rome

Picture Credits

Photographic credits appear in parentheses. The following abbreviations are used:
BON,V — Bildarchiv d. Ost. Nationalbibliothek, Vienna
HMSW — Historisches Museen der Stadt Wien
KM, V — Kunsthistorisches Museum, Vienna
(MEN) — (Marvin E. Newman)

ENDPAPERS Two engravings by W. H. Bartlett from William Beattie's *The Danube*, London, 1842. HALF TITLE Symbol by Jay J. Smith Studio. TITLE PAGE (MEN) 6–7 Francis & Shaw, Inc.

CHAPTER 1 9 top (MEN); bottom (Margot Granitsas) 10 Both: (Margot Granitsas) 10–11 (MEN) 11 (Margot Granitsas) 12–13 (MEN) 14 & 15 All: (MEN) 16–17 Tapestry of the Battle of Blenheim, 1704. His Grace the Duke of Marlborough (Jeremy Whitaker) 18 left (MEN); right, Monstrance commemorating the Battle of Lepanto, 1571, by Johann Zeckl, 1708. Maria de Victoria, Ingolstadt (MEN) 19 (MEN) 20–21 (MEN) 22 & 23 All: (MEN) 24 & 25 All: (MEN) 26 (MEN) 27 left (Bavaria-Verlag); right (MEN) 28–29 (MEN)

CHAPTER 2 31 Venus of Willendorf, *c.* 20,000 B.C. Naturhistorisches Museum, Vienna (Oronoz) 32 (Meyer) 33 Details from the Column of Marcus Aurelius, Rome. (Publifoto) 34 *Martyrdom of St. Florian*, by Albrecht Altdorfer. Narodni Gallery, Prague (Giraudon) 35 Alaric's signet ring. KM, V 36 Funeral stele, *c.* 700. Landesmuseum, Halle. 37 (Werkfoto) 38 & 39 (MEN) 40 German ivory of Otto I and the

Church of Magdeburg, 10th century. Metropolitan Museum of Art, gift of George Blumenthal, 1941. 41 Crown of St. Stephen. (Bildarchiv Foto Marburg) 42–43 (MEN) 44 Stained glass window of King Rudolf, 14th century. HMSW (Meyer)

CHAPTER 3 47 Woodcut of the Burgundian territories, from *The Triumphal Procession of Maximilian I* by Albrecht Altdorfer, 1516–18. 48 & 49 (MEN) 50 Francis & Shaw, Inc. 51 *Maximilian I and His Family*, by B. Striguel. Academia de San Fernando, Madrid (Oronoz) 52 *Suleiman the Magnificent*, by Nagari, 16th century. Topkapi Palace Museum (Ara Guler) 53 *The Battle of Mohács*, 1526. Topkapi Palace Museum (Ara Guler) 54 The horse ballet from Francesco Sbarra's *La Contessa dell'aria . . . Festa Cavallo . . .*, Vienna, 1667. Spencer Collection, New York Public Library 55 left, *Albrecht Furst Wallenstein*, by Schnorr von Carolsfeld after Anthony Van Dyke. Heeresgeschichtliches Museum, Vienna (Meyer); right, Anonymous painting of *The Thirty Years' War*. Kreuzkirche, Kreuz (Bavaria-Verlag) 56 Both: (MEN) 60–61 Anonymous painting of *The Turkish Seige of Vienna*, 1683. HMSW

CHAPTER 4 63 Ivory of Charles VI, by Matthias Steinle, 1711. KM, V (Meyer) 64 & 65 All: (MEN) 66 (Meyer) 66–67 *View of Vienna from the Belvedere*, by Bernardo Bellotto, 1759–60. KM, V (Meyer) 68–69 (MEN) 70 top left, Maria Theresa's jeweled bouquet by J. M. Grosser. KM, V (Meyer); top right, *Maria Theresa and Her Family*, by Martin von Meytens II, 1750. KM, V (Meyer); bottom, *The Damunkarusell*, by Martin von Meytens II, 1750. Schonbrunn Palace, Vienna (Meyer) 72 *Wolfgang Amadeus Mozart*, by Leonhard Posch, 1789. BON, V 73 *Ludwig van Beethoven*, by Feller after Lyser. Metropolitan Museum of Art, Crosby Brown Collection 74 Anonymous painting of *The Bombardment of Vienna*, 1809. Bibliothèque Nationale, Paris (Giraudon) 75 *The Congress of Vienna*, by J. B. Isabey, 1814. Bibliothèque Nationale, Paris 77 (Meyer) 78–79 (MEN) 80–81 *The Jagerzeile and the Leopoldstadtertheater*, Vienna, by Franz Schegerer, 1825. HMSW (Meyer) 83 *Barricade on the Michaelerplatz*, by Anton Ziegler, 1848. HMSW (Meyer)

CHAPTER 5 85 *Elizabeth and Franz Josef*, by Jakob Melcher, 1855. (Bavaria-Verlag) 86–87 *Panorama of Vienna*, by Gustav Veith, 1873. HMSW (Courtesy *Horizon Magazine*) 88 (MEN) 89 Both: Austrian National Tourist Office 90 (MEN) 92 The score of Johann Strauss' *The Blue Danube*, 1873. BON, V 92–93 *Franz Josef at the Hofball*, by von Wilhelm Gause, 1900 HMSW (Courtesy *Horizon Magazine*) 93 (MEN) 94–95 (MEN) 97 *Franz Josef Leaving the Hofburg Palace*, by Alexander Pock, 1910. BON, V (Courtesy *Horizon Magazine*) 98 top, Kaiserin Elizabeth, by G. Raab, 1873. Collection Fursten von Thrun-Taxis, Regensburg (Bavaria-Verlag); bottom, Katharine Schratt. BON, V 98 Franz Josef, 1916. BON, V 100 *Cafe Griensteidl*, by Reinhold Volkel, 1896. HMSW (Meyer) 101 (MEN) 102–03 *Market on the Danube Canal*, by Alois Schonn, 1895. HMSW (Meyer) 105 The Duchess and Archduke Ferdinand of Austria, Sarajevo, 1914. (UPI) 106–07 *The Attack on Belgrade*, by Oskar Laske. Heeresgeschichtliches Museum, Vienna (Meyer)

CHAPTER 6 109 Citizens in the Vienna Woods, 1919. BON, V 110 Adolf Hitler entering Vienna, 1938. BON, V 111 top, *A View of the Karlskirche*, by Adolf Hitler (Central Press Photos); bottom, *Vienna's Ringstrasse*, by Adolf Hitler (London Express) 112 & 113 All: (MEN) 114 (MEN) 116–17 (MEN) 118 (MEN)

CHAPTER 7 121 (MEN) 122 (MEN) 124–25 (MEN) 126 & 127 All: (MEN) 128 (AP) 129 (UPI) 131 (Georgio Nimatalleh) 132 Rumanian Tourist Office 133 (Bavaria-Verlag) 134–35 (Kurt Scholz, ZEFA) 135 (MEN) 136 (Margot Granitsas)

THE DANUBE IN LITERATURE 137–59 Twelve engravings by W.H. Bartlett from William Beattie's *The Danube*, London, 1842.

Index